CROSSROADS 4

STUDENT BOOK

Irene Frankel
Marjorie Fuchs

with

Earl W. Stevick

Oxford University Press

Acknowledgments

Thanks to the reviewers and consultants who helped shape this book:

Jayme Adelson-Goldstein, Los Angeles Unified School District, Los Angeles, California

Fiona Armstrong, New York City Board of Education, New York, New York

Martha F. Burns, North Hollywood Adult Learning Center, North Hollywood, California

Patty King, Los Angeles Unified School District, Los Angeles, California

Lorraine Luciano, United Education Institute, Santa Ana, California

Nancy Matthews, Language Training Institute, Englewood Cliffs, New Jersey

Cliff Meyers, University of Massachusetts, Amherst, Massachusetts

Joy Noren, Language Training Institute, Englewood Cliffs, New Jersey

Jack Wigfield, San Francisco City College, San Francisco, California

We'd like to thank our editors:

Susan Lanzano for so lovingly nurturing this project; Ken Mencz for his dedication to *Crossroads* and his unfailing patience and enthusiasm; and Allen Appel and Paul Phillips for taking care of the details. Thanks, too, to everyone else at Oxford, especially Jim O'Connor.

Thanks to the design team of Lynn Luchetti, Maj-Britt Hagsted, and Mary Martylewski for creating the unique look of *Crossroads*.

Thanks to those from whom we've learned so much about teaching ESL and teaching adults: Shirley Brod, Charles Curran, John Fanselow, Harvey Nadler, Jenny Rardin, Liz Steinberg, and Earl Stevick.

Thanks to Margot Gramer and Jenny Rardin for their unique contributions to this series.

This book is dedicated to our partners, David Martin and Rick Smith for always being there for us, to Irene's brother and his family — Evan Frankel, Rivalyn Zwieg, Zachary, and Chloe — and to Marjorie's family — Joseph Fuchs, Miriam Shakter, Gerry Seaman, and Gertrude Brooks — for all their love and support.

Contents

To the Teacher

Crossroads

- is a four-level adult series in English as a second language
- integrates a competency-based approach with systematic grammar presentation
- covers the four skills of listening, speaking, reading, and writing
- is for adults and young adults in adult or continuing education, or secondary programs
- begins lower and progresses more gradually than other beginning series
- provides an exceptionally complete and flexible array of classwork, homework, and teacher support materials through the Student Book, the Teacher's Book, Multilevel Activity and Resource Package, Workbook, Achievement Tests, and Cassettes

Level 4

The **Student Book** has ten units with the following sections:

Getting Started	provides a context for new material
Conversations	new competencies, grammar and vocabulary
Paperwork	document literacy
Reading and Writing	literacy skills
Listening Plus	listening skills
Interactions	information gap
Progress Checks	demonstration of competency

Practice conversations and the Listening Plus page are recorded on the **Cassettes.**

The **Teacher's Book** provides:

- warm-up activities
- step-by-step procedures for each exercise
- suggestions for varying and extending the exercises
- ways to teach pronunciation
- cross-cultural and linguistic notes
- reproducible versions of unit opener illustrations
- reproducible Competency Checklists

The **Multilevel Activity and Resource Package** is reproducible and includes:

- grammar and reading worksheets in two versions, for multilevel classes
- grammar focus and interactive listening worksheets
- pictures for language experience stories
- word and picture cards, games, and gameboards

- practical teaching notes
- *Crossroads* **Dictionary** and dictionary skills worksheets

The **Workbook** is designed for independent study and homework. It contains:

- grammar and reading worksheets in two versions, for multilevel classes
- grammar focus and writing worksheets
- answer key

Placement

Place students in CROSSROADS 1 if they function minimally or not at all in English.

Place students in CROSSROADS 2 if they are able to function in a very limited way, depending largely on learned phrases.

Place students in CROSSROADS 3 if they have moved beyond a limited range of learned phrases and are beginning to function with some independence and creativity, but still have difficulty communicating, even with someone who is used to dealing with people of limited English proficiency.

Place students in CROSSROADS 4 if they can communicate, although with some difficulty, on familiar topics with native speakers who are not accustomed to dealing with people of limited English proficiency.

CROSSROADS is compatible with the Comprehensive Adult Student Assessment System (CASAS) and the Student Performance Levels (SPL's) recommended by the Mainstream English Language Training (MELT) Project of the U.S. Department of Health and Human Services. SPL's are correlated with scores on the Basic English Skills Test (BEST).

	MELT SPL	BEST Score	CASAS Achievement Score
CROSSROADS 1	I and II	9–28	165–190
CROSSROADS 2	III	29–41	191–196
CROSSROADS 3	IV and V	42–57	197–210
CROSSROADS 4	VI and VII	58–65	211–224

Placement can also be made according to students' control of grammar. CROSSROADS 1 covers the present tense of *be,* the present continuous tense, and the simple present tense. CROSSROADS 2 covers the past tense of *be* and regular verbs, and the future with *be going to.* CROSSROADS 3 covers the past tense with irregular verbs, the future tense with *will*, and the past progressive tense. CROSSROADS 4 covers the present perfect and present perfect continuous tenses.

| a | b | c | ... |

One of these symbols in the margin next to an exercise tells you that a specific competency is first practiced there. In the Progress Checks pages, the same letter identifies the exercise that tests that competency.

Teaching Procedures

An underlying principle of CROSSROADS is *elicit before you teach.* We suggest that students guess what the text might say, share any language they already know about the topic, listen to the text on cassette or as read by their teacher, and learn or review key vocabulary. Similarly, before attempting independent pair practice, students might repeat the exercise aloud together, learn needed vocabulary, and participate in supervised pair practice.

Most instruction lines recur throughout the book and stand for, rather than spell out, complete teaching procedures. **Step-by-Step Teaching Procedures** for these recurring exercises appear on pages vii–xi, following this introduction. They state the purpose of the exercise and include preparation and follow-up steps to help students progress at their own pace.

Most exercises are covered by the Step-by-Step Teaching Procedures. Those that are not are covered in the Teacher's Book, which provides an individually tailored procedure for every Student Book exercise.

Many of the exercises in CROSSROADS ask students to provide information about themselves. Most students enjoy this and feel that it helps them learn. However, there may be times when students are unwilling or unable to supply personal information. Therefore, some of the teaching procedures suggest that students may provide fictitious rather than true information.

Progress Checks

The last two pages of each unit are *Progress Checks,* which allow you and the students to find out how well they have mastered the competencies presented in the unit. Even if your program is not competency-based, these exercises provide a useful way for students to demonstrate that they have acquired the language taught in the unit.

Each exercise tests a specific competency or competencies, identified by letter and by name. You can evaluate students yourself, have peers evaluate each other, or have students evaluate themselves. Reproducible Competency Checklists in the back of

the Teacher's Book can help with record-keeping.

The two-part exercises called *What are the people saying? / Do it yourself* are unique to Crossroads. In *What are the people saying?,* students work in pairs or alone to generate a conversation based on what they have practiced in the unit. They are prompted by pictures, and some of the words and sentences may be supplied. This first part of the exercise provides a review of what students have practiced, and also lets them demonstrate how well they control the grammatical structures involved. *What are the people saying?* can be done just orally, or followed up with writing. An Answer Key for *What are the people saying?* appears in the back of the Student Book. The second part of the exercise, *Do it yourself,* is where competency is demonstrated.

When a competency requires reading *(Read notices from a school, Read housing ads),* the needed reading material is provided in the exercise. Progress Checks are designed for classroom use, but most competencies are actually needed outside of the classroom, in the community. For this reason, *Do it yourself* sometimes involves a degree of role play and imagination. For example, to demonstrate the competency *Fill in a medical history form,* students fill in a facsimile of a doctor's or clinic's intake form. When appropriate, students are given the opportunity to test their competency in real life situations outside of the classroom.

Culminating Activities

Each unit of Student Book 4 ends with a *Problem Solving* exercise, culminating in a role play. As a group, students discuss problems which they are likely to encounter in daily life in the United States. These activities encourage students to draw upon all of their communicative resources and to exercise their creativity.

Problem Solving is not an evaluation tool like other exercises on the Progress Checks pages. It provides an opportunity for the students to bring their new language skills to bear on a fairly complex and extended task. Success is in completion of the task, rather than in accurate production of language.

Grammar Summary, Tapescript, Useful Irregular Verbs

These three sections, together with the Answer Key for Progress Checks mentioned above, are located in the back of the Student Book.

The Grammar Summary presents complete paradigms of grammatical structures practiced in the Student Book, including those highlighted in *Focus on grammar* exercises. The Tapescript for Listening Plus lets you preview exercises and to read them aloud if the Cassette is not available. Useful Irregular Verbs includes 95 of the most frequently used irregular verbs in their base, past, and perfect forms.

Step-by-Step Teaching Procedures
(in order of appearance)

GETTING STARTED
Guess.

Provides a context for the unit.
1. Give students a little time to look at the picture.
2. Have students identify the characters, or identify them yourself.
3. Ask where the characters are.
4. Ask students to guess what the characters are doing.
5. Ask students to guess what the characters are saying. All responses are valid here.
6. Ask students to guess what's going to happen next.
7. Respond to each guess by restating it in acceptable English.

What can you hear?

Prepares students for the first conversation on the next page.
1. Have students look at the picture while you play the tape or read the conversation aloud.
2. Have students volunteer any words, phrases, or sentences they can recall from the conversation.
3. Acknowledge all contributions by restating them in acceptable English. Write them on the board.

CONVERSATIONS
Practice. (the first conversation in the unit)

Introduces specific competencies, grammar, and/or vocabulary.
1. Have students compare the words, phrases, or sentences on the board (from *What can you hear?*) with the conversations in the book.
2. Play the tape or read the conversation aloud while students follow along silently in their books.
3. Use the pictures on the previous page or otherwise elicit or demonstrate the meaning of key words and phrases.
4. Have students repeat the conversation chorally and then practice in pairs.

Add two words/phrases with similar meanings.

Provides for vocabulary expansion based on what students collectively know.
1. Write the words or phrases from the book on the board or overhead projector. Have students underline the words or phrases in the conversation.
2. Have students work in small groups to come up with words or phrases with similar meanings. Circulate to help. Allow students to use dictionaries if they wish.
3. Have students write their group's answers on the board.
4. Have students edit the answers for spelling, grammar, and appropriateness.

Focus on grammar.

Helps students infer grammatical principles without using grammar terms.
1. Choose a pair of items that contrast. (*My sister drove a bus. She didn't drive a truck.*) Write the pair side by side on the board or overhead projector.
2. Read the two items aloud and have students repeat.
3. Provide another example like the left-hand item. (*I went to Japan.*) Write it underneath and have students repeat.
4. Elicit the corresponding item for the right-hand column. (*I didn't go to Korea.*) Write it and have students repeat.
5. Point to the next space in the right-hand column and elicit an example to fill it.
6. Elicit the corresponding item for the left-hand column.
7. Have students copy the items on a separate piece of paper.
8. Use the same procedure for the other contrasting pairs in the exercise.

Practice. (after the first one in the unit)

Introduces specific competencies, grammar, and/or vocabulary.
1. Play the tape or read the conversation aloud while students follow along silently in their books.
2. Ask students to set the scene, saying who the characters are, where they are, and what they are doing.
3. Elicit or demonstrate the meaning of key words and phrases.
4. Play the tape again and ask questions to check comprehension.
5. Have students repeat the conversation chorally and then practice in pairs.

Talk about _____ .

Provides practice with competencies, grammar, and vocabulary.
1. Read the conversation aloud and have students repeat.
2. Elicit the meaning of any new vocabulary items (or explain them yourself if none of the students can). Once the meaning is clear, have students repeat the new vocabulary.
3. Have two volunteers say the conversation for the class, making appropriate substitutions.
4. Have students practice the conversation in pairs, changing partners, saying both parts, and using all the information.

Talk about your_____ / yourself.

Provides personalized practice with competencies, grammar, and vocabulary.

Note: In some of these exercises, students may want or need to give fictitious information about themselves. Tell students that this is acceptable.

1. Read the conversation aloud and have students repeat. Then have a volunteer say the conversation with you; provide information about yourself where needed.
2. Have two volunteers say the conversation for the class, providing their personal information where needed.
3. Have students practice the conversation in pairs. Then have them change partners and roles.

PAPERWORK

Read _____ . Circle a word you want to learn. Work with your classmates. Find out what it means.

Introduces vocabulary for these documents.
1. Have students read the text silently and circle the one word they most want to learn.
2. Call on students to say (or spell) their circled words. Pronounce the words and write them on the board or overhead projector.
3. Ask if anyone can explain what any of the words means. Encourage students to contribute until everyone understands the meanings. Allow students to use dictionaries. Supply explanations yourself as a last resort.
4. Continue the process until all circled words have been explained.
5. Have students read the text again.
6. Ask simple questions to check comprehension and confirm students' understanding of the vocabulary. (*What words mean* the day you came to the U.S.? *Which words mean* the reason you are taking this class?)

Add questions with your classmates. Then interview three classmates.

Lets students exchange personal information.

Note: Students may want or need to give fictitious information about themselves. Tell students that this is acceptable.

1. Copy the questions on the board or overhead projector. Have a student ask you the first question. Give the answer in the example, and write it on the board.
2. Have volunteers ask and answer the other questions.
3. Invite students to contribute additional questions based on the document in Exercise 1. Write their questions on the board and have the class correct any errors.
4. Say all the questions one at a time and have students repeat. Have students copy the questions on a separate piece of paper.
5. Have volunteers ask and answer the questions for the class.
6. Have students work in groups of four to ask each other the questions and write the answers.

Pool your information. Then write summary sentences.

Provides collaborative practice in collecting and summarizing information.
1. Write the questions from Exercise 3 on the board or overhead projector.
2. Have each group from Exercise 3 choose a secretary. Have each secretary write his group's answers (including his own) on the board.
3. Direct the class to tally the information (e.g., *8–Spanish, 6–Vietnamese, 3–Khmer, 2–Russian, and 1–Korean*).
4. Model the first summary sentence (e.g., *Eight students speak Spanish as a first language, six students speak Vietnamese, etc.*) and write it on the board.
5. Repeat the process with the other questions, letting students volunteer the summary statements. Have the class correct any mistakes.
6. Have students copy the summary statements in paragraph form.

READING AND WRITING

Read _____. Circle a word you want to learn. Work with your classmates. Find out what it means.

Provides practice in reading connected discourse. Provides a cooperative process for learning new vocabulary.
1. Have students read the text silently and circle the one word they most want to learn.

2. Call on students to say (or spell) their circled words. Pronounce the words and write them on the board or overhead projector.
3. Ask if anyone can explain what any of the words mean. Encourage students to contribute until everyone understands the meanings. Allow students to use dictionaries. Supply explanations yourself as a last resort.
4. Continue the process until all circled words have been explained.
5. Have students read the text again.
6. Ask questions to check comprehension. (*How often should an adult take "Cold Arrest"? What should you do in case of an accidental overdose?*)

Write in your journal
Compare _____ in the United States and in your country.

Provides an opportunity for writing about cross-cultural experiences.

Note: Journal writing is an optional writing activity intended to encourage students to express their ideas and feelings freely in writing without worrying about grammatical, mechanical, or rhetorical correctness. The topic provided is a suggestion only. The following is one way to use the exercise.

1. Read the instructions aloud.
2. Have students talk to each other about the topic in pairs for a few minutes. Ask a few students to share their ideas with the whole class.
3. Have students write about the topic for ten minutes (or have students write for ten minutes at home). Have students fold their papers in half lengthwise and write on the left side of the paper only.
4. To encourage students to write more fluently, don't correct the writing. Instead, respond only to the content of the journal, writing brief comments or questions on the right side of the page.

LISTENING PLUS
Listen to the contrast. Point.

Helps students distinguish differences in meaning based on differences in stress and intonation.

Listen to the contrast.

1. Write the column headings and sample sentences on the board or overhead projector.
2. Have students notice whether the sentences are written identically or are punctuated differently.
3. Ask students to listen to the differences in the sentences as you play the tape or read the sentences aloud.
4. Elicit the differences in stress or intonation (e.g., *in the first one, your voice goes down at the end, but in the second one, it goes up*). Elicit the

differences in meaning (e.g., *in the first one, you're making a statement, but in the second one, you're asking a question*).

Point.

1. Write the two column headings on the board.
2. Play the tape or read the tapescript aloud, sentence by sentence. Have students point to the column headings in their books.
3. Play the tape or read the tapescript aloud again while a volunteer points to the correct column heading at the board so students can check their answers.

Number the pictures.

Gives practice in listening for gist.

Note: In this exercise, students may hear short conversations beyond the level they are expected to produce or even completely understand.

1. Have students look at each of the four illustrations and tell you what's going on in each one.
2. Play the tape or read the tapescript aloud as many times as students need. Have students number the illustrations from 1 to 4 to match what they hear on the tape.
3. Have students compare their answers in pairs.
4. Draw four boxes on the board or overhead projector corresponding to the illustrations in the text.
5. Play the tape or read the tapescript again, one conversation at a time. After each conversation, have a volunteer write the number in the appropriate box and say what she heard that gave her the answer.
6. Let students hear the conversations once more to verify their answers.

What do you think the next speaker will say?

Gives practice in predicting what is likely to be said next in a conversation.

1. Play the first conversation again or read the tapescript aloud. Have students think about what the next speaker might say.
2. Have students write their guesses on a separate piece of paper.
3. Let students hear the conversation again to see how their answers work.
4. Have students work in pairs to compare answers. (There will be more than one appropriate answer.)
5. Have several volunteers put their answers on the board and play the conversation again. Have the class decide which answers are valid.
6. Repeat for the other conversations.

INTERACTIONS

Before you get or give information . . .

Allows students to have input into or otherwise prepare for the information gap activity that follows.

1. Review vocabulary students will need in the exercise.
2. Show students that there are two pages. Divide the class into a Student A group and a Student B. Have them each open their books to the appropriate page.
3. Have students follow the instructions. Circulate and give help as needed.
4. If appropriate, have A's work with other A's and B's work with other B's to check their answers.

Get information./Give information.

Provides an information gap activity for communicative practice.

1. Review A's and B's tasks for the information gap.
2. Call on a volunteer from each group to model the conversation for the class.
3. Have them (or two other volunteers) ask and answer the next question. Check that the class is clear about the task.
4. Review vocabulary if necessary.
5. Have A's work with B's to do the task and fill in the information. Then have them compare their pages to check their answers.
6. As an option, have students change roles and do both pages.

PROGRESS CHECKS

What are the people saying?/Do it yourself.

Provides for demonstration of competency.

What are the people saying?

1. Have students work in pairs to identify the situation, the relationship of the people, and what the people are saying. Circulate to give help and feedback.
2. Have students generate the conversations in the bubbles, either individually or with partners, orally or in writing.
3. Have a pair or group of volunteers act out the conversation for the class. Have the other students approve what they say or suggest changes.

Do it yourself.

1. Have students say the conversation with a partner, using their own information and/or whatever cues are supplied. Then have students change roles and say it again.

2. When a student has successfully demonstrated a competency, it can be checked off, dated, or initialed.

PROBLEM SOLVING

What's _____ 's problem?
What should _____ do?

Lets students apply their experience to group problem-solving activities.

What's _____ 's problem?

1. Have students work in pairs or small groups for a few minutes to describe the problem in the illustration. If necessary, prompt students by asking a few questions.
2. Call on volunteers to speak for their groups. Write all suggestions on the board or overhead projector.
3. Have the class discuss which statements best describe the problem.

What should _____ do?

1. Have the students return to their groups to discuss what the character(s) should do. Groups may come up with more than one solution.
2. Call on volunteers to speak for their groups. Write all suggestions on the board or overhead projector.
3. Have the class discuss which solutions they like best, giving reasons for their choices. Some solutions may be culturally inappropriate in the United States. Explain why.

Now role play.

Provides an opportunity for creative language use.

1. Have volunteers take the parts of the characters.
2. Have them "perform" the whole story with one of the suggested solutions.
3. Have students discuss the outcome. Was the problem solved?

Debra Richard's Level 4 Class

1 Introductions

Getting Started _____

1. **Guess. Where are Debra and Li-Wu? What are they doing? What are they saying? What are they going to do next?**

2. **What can you hear?**

Conversations

 1. Practice.

Debra: Hello. My name is Debra Richards.
Li-Wu: I'm Li-Wu Chen.
Debra: I'm sorry. I didn't catch your name.
Li-Wu: It's Li-Wu Chen.
Debra: Nice to meet you, Mr. Chen.
Li-Wu: Nice to meet you, too, Ms. Richards.
Debra: Oh, you can call me Debra.
Li-Wu: OK. And please call me Chen.

2. Meet five classmates. Use the conversation in 1.

3. Practice.

Manny: Carlos, I'd like you to meet Meng Hut.
Meng, this is Carlos ....
I'm sorry, Carlos, I forgot your last name.
Carlos: It's Vega.
Manny: Oh, that's right. Vega.
Meng, this is Carlos Vega.
Meng: Glad to meet you.
Carlos: Glad to meet you, too.
Your first name is Meng?
Meng: Right.

4. Introduce two classmates. Use the conversation in 3.

5. Add two phrases with similar meanings.

I'm sorry. I didn't catch your name.   *Nice to meet you.*

<u>Excuse me. Can you repeat your name, please?</u>

_____   _____

 6. Practice.

Meng: Where are you from, Carlos?
Carlos: Honduras.
Meng: Oh. What did you do there?
Carlos: I was a bus driver. I drove a school bus. What about you?
Meng: I'm from Cambodia. I was a teacher there.
Carlos: When did you come to the United States?
Meng: Four years ago. But we came to Bridgeton just last year.

Conversations _____

7. Focus on grammar. Review.

My sister	drove	a bus.
I	went	to Japan.

She	didn't	drive	a truck.
I		go	to Korea.

Did	she	drive	a school bus?
	you	go	to Taiwan?

When		did	she	drive a bus?
What countries			you	go to?

8. Talk about the students.

A: What did ___Lucy___ do in ___Mexico___?

B: ___She___ was a ___factory worker___. ___She made clothes___.

A: When did ___she___ come here?

B: ___She___ came here ___in 1991___.

Lucy/Mexico
factory worker
make clothes
in 1991

Marco/Brazil
student
go to the university
three years ago

Manny/the Philippines
construction worker
build roads
last year

Sonia/Mexico
farmer
grow vegetables
in 1982

Li-Wu/Taiwan
paramedic
drive an ambulance
in 1989

9. Find out about five classmates. Use the conversation in 6.

Conversations _____

10. Practice.

Lucy: Who's that guy over there?
        He's really good-looking.
Anda: That's Marco Veltman. He was
        in my class last year.
Lucy: He was in your class?
        What's he like?
Anda: Well, he's very intelligent
        and a wonderful cook.
Lucy: He sounds interesting.
Anda: Come on. I'll introduce you.

11. Add two words with similar meanings.

good-looking	*intelligent*	*wonderful*
nice-looking		

12. Play the Name Game.

**13. Talk about your classmates. Use the conversation in 10 and
your imagination.**

Paperwork _____

1. **Read the form. Circle a word you want to learn. Work with your classmates. Find out what it means.**

Westside Community Adult School

DATE ☐☐ – ☐☐ – ☐☐

☐ Mr. ☐ Ms.
☐ Mrs. ☐ Miss

Last name ☐☐☐☐☐☐☐☐☐☐☐☐☐ First name ☐☐☐☐☐☐☐ Middle name ☐☐☐☐☐☐☐

ADDRESS

Number ☐☐☐☐ Street ☐☐☐☐☐☐☐☐☐☐☐☐☐☐☐☐ Apt. ☐☐☐

City ☐☐☐☐☐☐☐☐☐☐☐☐☐☐☐☐ State ☐☐ ZIP ☐☐☐☐☐ – ☐☐☐☐

DAYTIME PHONE ☐☐☐ – ☐☐☐ – ☐☐☐☐

EVENING PHONE ☐☐☐ – ☐☐☐ – ☐☐☐☐

Place of Birth _____ Date of Birth _____

Date of Arrival in U.S. _____ First Language _____

Last grade completed _____ _____ _____
                          Grade   Year   Location

Educational Goal   ☐ U.S. Citizenship   ☐ Get a job   ☐ Get a better job   ☐ GED

☐ Other _____

Need practice in   ☐ Listening   ☐ Speaking   ☐ Reading

☐ Writing   ☐ Grammar   ☐ Vocabulary

---

d 2. **Fill in the form for yourself.**

3. **Add questions with your classmates. Then interview three classmates.**

What's your first language?	Spanish
When did you come to the U.S.?	1991
Why do you want to improve your English?	to get a GED
_____?	_____

4. **Pool your information. Then write summary sentences.**

Reading and Writing _____

1. **You're going to read Debra Richard's autobiography. With your books closed, work in pairs and write 5 to 8 words you think you may find in her story.**

2. **Read Debra's autobiography. Circle a word you want to learn. Work with your classmates. Find out what it means.**

 I was born in 1955 in Madison, Wisconsin. My mother was an accountant and my father worked in the dairy industry. I grew up with my two older brothers and one younger sister. When I was ten, my father died. Then we moved to Bridgeton, where my grandparents lived.

I graduated from high school in 1973. Then I went to college and studied Spanish. In my junior year, I went to Spain to study. After college, I went to Colombia to teach English. I met my husband there. He was also a teacher.

Two years later, we came back to the United States and got married. Then I got a job teaching English as a second language in Bridgeton. In 1983, my son Andy was born. I took off a year from work.

Three years later, my husband and I got divorced. The year after that, I got an extra job teaching part-time at the Westside Community Adult School. I really like teaching adults.

3. **Read the autobiography again. How many of your words are in it?**

4. **Work in pairs. Underline all the time expressions. Then complete the timeline for Debra.**

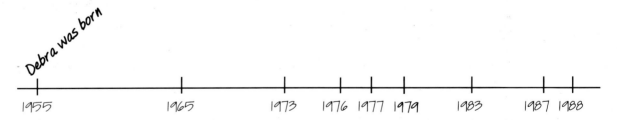

5. **Write a timeline for yourself. Talk about it with your partner. Then write your autobiography. Use Debra's autobiography as an example.**

6. **Read your autobiography to your group.**

Reading and Writing _____

7. **Debra asked the students to compare introductions in their countries and the United States. First, she gave them a worksheet. Look at Keiyu's.**

ESL Level 4	Comparing Introductions	Name: Keiyu Takada

Step 1: **Choose one from each column:**

People	Ages	Situation
☐ a man and a woman	☐ one older, one younger	☐ a party
☐ two women	☒ about the same age	☒ an office
☒ two men		☐ a class

Step 2: **Answer these questions about the people when they first meet.**

	Your Country: Japan	the U.S.
a. Do they give their full names?	No	Yes
b. Do they make eye contact?	Yes	Yes
c. Do they shake hands or bow?	Bow	Shake hands
d. Do they smile?	Yes	Yes
e. Do they call each other by their first names?	No	Yes
f. What else do they do?	Exchange business cards	

8. **Next, Debra asked the students to write in their journals. Read Keiyu's.**

> In Japan, when men of the same age meet for the first time at an office, they tell each other their last names. They make eye contact. They bow and smile. They call each other by their last names and add the word "san," which means Mr. They always exchange business cards when they first meet. This is very important.

> In the U.S., when men of the same age meet for the first time at an office, they tell each other their full names. They make eye contact. They shake hands and smile. They usually call each other by their first names. They sometimes exchange business cards, but not until they say goodbye.

9. **Write in your journal. Compare introductions in your country and in the U.S. Use the worksheet in 7 and the journal in 8 as examples.**

Listening Plus _____

1. Listen to the contrast. Point.

Statement	**Question**
He was in her class.	He was in her class?

Write a period (.) or question mark (?) at the end of each sentence.

1. She was in his class __
2. That's our teacher __
3. He sold cars __
4. They met in 1991 __
5. They're from Mexico __
6. She was a doctor __

2. Listen. Number the pictures.

Listen again. What do you think the next speaker will say?

3. You are the secretary at the Westside Community Adult School. Play the messages on the school's answering machine. Fill in the information.

Name: _____
Day: _____
Time: _____
Phone No.: _____

Name: _____
Day: _____
Time: _____
Phone No.: _____

Name: _____
Day: _____
Time: _____
Phone No.: _____

Interactions _____
Student A

1. **Before you get or give information, read about Danny, a new student at the Westside Community Adult School. Use your imagination and complete his biography.**

> Danny was born in 1954 in Hong Kong. He lived in a small house with his grandparents, his parents, his two brothers, and his sister. He graduated from high school in 19____. Then he went to work in a bicycle factory.
>
> Danny wanted a better job, and he enrolled in evening classes in 19____. He met his wife, Monica, in his English class. Danny and Monica got married in 19____. ____ years later, they had a baby boy. ____ years after their son was born, they had a second child, a girl. When the girl was ____ years old, they moved to Bridgeton, California.
>
> Life was difficult for Danny and Monica. They didn't speak much English and they didn't know many people. Danny got a job in a factory, and Monica stayed home with the children. In 19____, Danny enrolled in English classes at the Westside Community Adult School.

2. **Get information. Ask B about Ana, another new student. Fill in the years on the timeline.**

   A: When was Ana born?

   B: In 1960.

   A: ___Was that '50 or '60___?

   B: '60.

   A: When did she ___graduate from high school___?

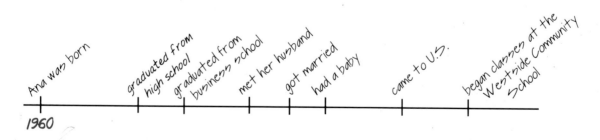

3. **Give information. Answer B's questions about Danny.**

4. **Find out about important dates in your partner's life.**

Interactions _____
Student B

1. **Before you get or give information, read about Ana, a new student at the Westside Community Adult School. Use your imagination and complete her biography.**

Ana was born in 1960 in Caracas, Venezuela. She lived in a small house with her parents, her brother, and her sister. She graduated from high school in 19____. Then she went to business school, and she graduated ____ years later.

Ana got a job as a secretary in a hotel in 19____. She met her husband, Wilfredo, there; he was a desk clerk. They got married in 19____. The next year, they had a baby girl, Alba. When Alba was ____ years old, they moved to Bridgeton, California.

Life was difficult for Ana and Wilfredo. They didn't speak much English and they didn't know many people. Ana got a job as a housekeeper during the day, and Wilfredo got a job in a restaurant at night. In 19____, they enrolled in English classes at the Westside Community Adult School.

2. **Give information. Answer A's questions about Ana.**

   A: When was Ana born?

   B: In 1960.

   A: _Was that '50 or '60_____?

   B: '60.

   A: When did she _graduate from high school_____?

3. **Get information. Ask A about Danny, another new student. Fill in the years on the timeline.**

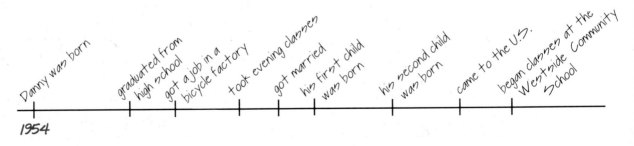

4. **Find out about important dates in your partner's life.**

Progress Checks ✔

1. **d** ☐ Fill in a form with personal information.

Fill in the form.

NAME	*First* ☐☐☐☐☐☐☐☐☐	*Middle* ☐☐☐☐☐☐☐☐	*Last* ☐☐☐☐☐☐☐☐☐☐☐☐	

ADDRESS	*Number* ☐☐☐☐☐	*Street* ☐☐☐☐☐☐☐☐☐☐☐☐☐☐☐☐		*Apt.* ☐☐☐☐
	City ☐☐☐☐☐☐☐☐☐☐☐☐☐☐☐☐☐☐		*State* ☐☐	*ZIP* ☐☐☐☐☐–☐☐☐☐

HOME PHONE ☐☐☐–☐☐☐–☐☐☐☐   **WORK PHONE** ☐☐☐–☐☐☐–☐☐☐☐

FIRST LANGUAGE ☐☐☐☐☐☐☐☐☐☐   **PLACE OF BIRTH** ☐☐☐☐☐☐☐☐☐☐

LAST GRADE COMPLETED	*Grade* ☐☐☐☐	*Year* ☐☐☐☐	*Country* ☐☐☐☐☐☐☐☐☐☐☐☐☐☐☐☐

2. **a** ☐ Introduce yourself.
   b ☐ Ask someone to repeat a part of a conversation.
   c ☐ Introduce other people.

What are the people saying?

Do it yourself.

Progress Checks ✔

3. **e** ☐   Give details about your personal background.

What are the people saying?

Do it yourself.

Problem Solving

What's the problem?

What should Linda say?
Now role play.
What kinds of problems have you had at parties?

2 Transportation

Getting Started _____

1. Guess. Where are Meng and the police officer? What are they doing?
    What are they saying? What's going to happen next?

2. What can you hear?

Conversations _____

1. **Practice.**

> Officer: I'll be with you in a moment, sir. Now, ma'am, what happened?
> Meng: Well, I was driving south on 10th Avenue when the gray car ran the stop sign and hit me.
> Officer: And how fast were you going?
> Meng: Fortunately, only 25 miles an hour. But he was doing at least 40.
> Officer: Were you wearing your seat belt?
> Meng: Yes, I always do.

2. **Focus on grammar. Review.**

Pat and Sue	were wearing their seat belts	when	the yellow car hit them.
The blue car	was doing at least 40		the accident happened.

3. **Talk about the accidents.**

A: What happened?

B: The ___white___ car was going ___south___ on ___10th Avenue___ when the ___gray___ car ___ran the stop sign___.

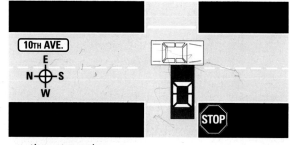

run the stop sign

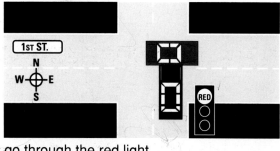

go through the red light

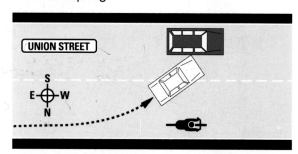

swerve into the next lane

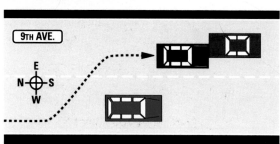

try to pass

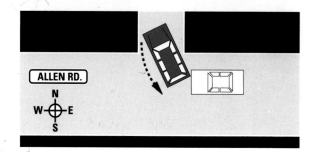

back out of the driveway

Conversations _____

a 4. Pretend you had one of the accidents in 3. Talk about your accident. Use the conversation in 1.

5. Practice.

Man:	Did you see what happened?
Woman:	Yeah. That guy didn't stop.
Man:	He ran right through that stop sign?
Woman:	Yeah. He drives worse than my Uncle Jim.
Man:	Look at his car. I bet he'll drive more carefully next time.

6. Focus on grammar.

slowly carefully dangerously	more	slowly carefully dangerously	than

fast well badly	faster better worse	than

7. Talk about Meng and Don. Use the words in 6 and the driving records below.

A: Who drives _____more slowly_____, Meng or Don?

B: ___Meng___ drives ____more slowly____ than ___Don___.

STATE OF CALIFORNIA

DMV
DEPARTMENT OF MOTOR VEHICLES

DRIVING RECORD

NAME: Hut   Meng
      Last   First

PARKING VIOLATIONS:
* Parking in a no-parking area

MOVING VIOLATIONS:
* None

EQUIPMENT VIOLATIONS:
* Driving with a broken left headlight

STATE OF CALIFORNIA

DMV
DEPARTMENT OF MOTOR VEHICLES

DRIVING RECORD

NAME: Anderson   Don
      Last   First

PARKING VIOLATIONS:
* Parking in front of a fire hydrant

MOVING VIOLATIONS:
* Speeding -- 70 mph in a 55 mph zone
* Made an illegal U-turn
* Speeding -- 45 mph in a school zone

EQUIPMENT VIOLATIONS:
* None

Conversations _____

8. Practice.

Manny: I'm glad you're all right, Meng.
Meng: Thanks, Manny. But my car is
         a wreck. The front is crushed and
         the engine is badly damaged.
Manny: That's too bad. Are you going
         to get a new car?
Meng: Well, not new, used.

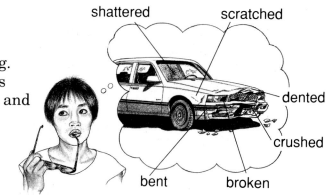

9. Add two words or phrases with similar meanings.

a wreck	*That's too bad.*
a mess	

10. Talk about the cars. Use the words below and the words in 8.

A: Is the blue car badly damaged?

B: Yes. The roof is crushed and a rear fender is dented.

    What about the black car?

A: A door is scratched and the windshield is shattered.

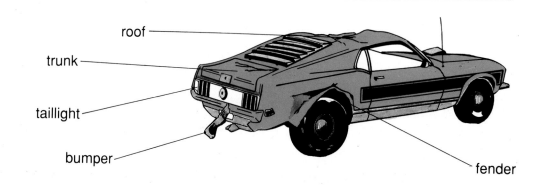

Paperwork

1. **Read the used car ads. Circle a word you want to learn. Work with your classmates. Find out what it means.**

THE DAILY TRIBUNE   26 D

89 DODGE COLT GT	90 FORD ESCORT GT	87 TOYOTA CAMRY
5 spd trans, 40M, gd cond, 36 mpg, am-fm ster, $4500 – orig owner, call weekends (209) 569-3541	pb, ps, pw, pdl, air, xlnt cond, extended wrnty, 27M, $6100 obo (209) 798-1179	2 dr, auto trans, perf cond, gray w blue int, am-fm cass, lo mi, $3500 (209) 537-4972
89 CADILLAC gd cond	92 SUBARU auto trans,	81 VOLKSWAGEN 4

C

2. **Write the abbreviations from 1 for these words.**

1. air-conditioning _air_	9. thousand ____	17. power steering ____
2. automatic ____	10. mileage ____	18. power windows ____
3. cassette ____	11. miles per gallon ____	19. speed ____
4. condition ____	12. or best offer ____	20. stereo ____
5. door ____	13. original ____	21. transmission ____
6. good ____	14. power brakes ____	22. with ____
7. interior ____	15. perfect ____	23. warranty ____
8. low ____	16. power door locks ____	24. excellent ____

3. **Add questions with your classmates. Then interview three classmates.**

Do you have a driver's license?   _yes_

What options would you like on a new car?   _5 speed transmission,_
                                                                      air-conditioning

What's the make and model of your favorite car?   _Chevy Corvette_

_____?   _____

4. **Pool your information. Then write summary sentences.**

Reading and Writing _____

1. **Work in pairs. With your books closed, write a list of things you should do if you have a car accident.**

2. **Read the information from the Department of Motor Vehicles. Circle a word you want to learn. Work with your classmates. Find out what it means.**

IF YOU ARE IN AN ACCIDENT:

■ STOP. You must stop if your car is in an accident.

■ Move your car out of the traffic lanes, if you can.

■ Call the police immediately if anyone is hurt or killed. The police officer will write a report of the accident.

CALLING FOR HELP

■ Dial 911. The call is free.

■ Give the location of the accident.

■ Give your name and the phone number you are calling from.

■ DO NOT HANG UP! Wait for the emergency operator to end the call.

■ Give your name and address to the other driver.

■ Show your driver's license and registration card to the other driver.

■ Make a full written report to the Department of Moter Vehicles within 10 days if anyone is injured or killed or if there is more than $500 of property damage.

---

3. **Read the information again. How much of this information was on your list?**

4. **Work in pairs. Correct these statements.**

    a. You should wait for the police before you move your car.
        You should move your car if you can.

    b. You should call the police within 24 hours if anyone is hurt or killed.
    c. You should give your home phone number to the emergency operator.
    d. You should show your driver's license and registration to the police only.
    e. You have to file a report with the Department of Motor Vehicles if there is property damage of $400.

Reading and Writing _____

5. **Read the accident report Meng filed with her insurance company.**

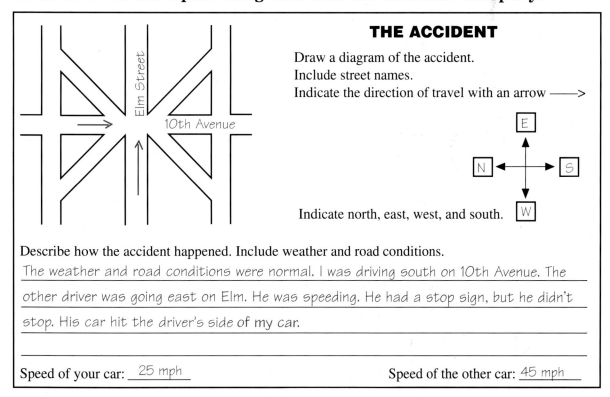

THE ACCIDENT

Draw a diagram of the accident.
Include street names.
Indicate the direction of travel with an arrow ———>

Indicate north, east, west, and south.

Describe how the accident happened. Include weather and road conditions.

The weather and road conditions were normal. I was driving south on 10th Avenue. The other driver was going east on Elm. He was speeding. He had a stop sign, but he didn't stop. His car hit the driver's side of my car.

Speed of your car: _25 mph_   Speed of the other car: _45 mph_

6. **Look at the diagram. Talk about the accident with a partner.**

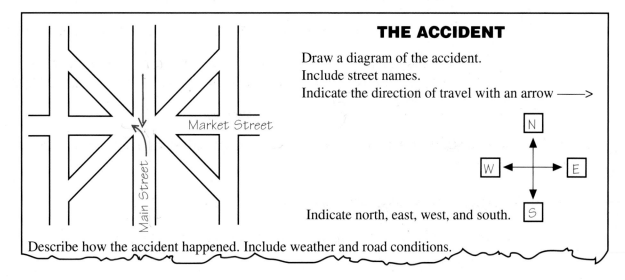

THE ACCIDENT

Draw a diagram of the accident.
Include street names.
Indicate the direction of travel with an arrow ———>

Indicate north, east, west, and south.

Describe how the accident happened. Include weather and road conditions.

d **7.** **Complete the accident report in 6. Use Meng's accident report as an example. Then read your accident report to your group.**

8. **Write in your journal. Compare driving in the United States and in your country.**

Listening Plus _____

1. Listen to the contrast. Point.

Statement	**Question**
He drove right through that stop sign.	He drove right through that stop sign?

Write a period (.) or question mark (?) at the end of each sentence.

1. Marta got a new car __

2. Bill is a good driver __

3. It's $20,000 __

4. It was the blue car's fault __

5. His car broke down __

6. There's an accident up ahead __

2. Listen. Number the pictures.

Listen again. What do you think the next speaker will say?

3. You want to travel from Bridgeton to San Diego tomorrow afternoon. Call Caltrak Railways. Use the keypad. Instead of pushing a button, check (√) it. Fill in the information in the boxes.

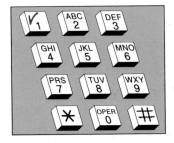

Leave Bridgeton	Arrive San Diego

Cost
One-way:
Round-trip:

Interactions _____

Student A

1. **Before you get or give information, use your imagination and complete the car ads.**

89 MERCURY TOPAZ, _____ M
ps, pb, auto, air, am-fm cass, 1 yr extended
wrnty, _____ MPG, _____ dr, xlnt cond,
orig owner, $_____

87 VOLKSWAGEN JETTA, red,
_____ spd, perf cond, _____ M,
pw, pdl, new tires, air, orig owner, _____
MPG, $_____ obo

2. **Get information. B put two used car notices on a bulletin board. Call and write the information about B's used cars.**

    A: I'm calling about the _‛88 Buick Regal_ for sale.

    B: Yes. It's a great buy.

    A: What's the mileage?

    B: __42,000 miles__ .

    A: _____?

FOR SALE
‛88 BUICK REGAL

FOR SALE
‛89 FORD TEMPO GLS

	'88 Buick Regal	'89 Ford Tempo GLS
Mileage?	42,000 miles	
Original owner?		
Miles per gallon?		
Problems?		
Options?		
Price?		
_____?		

3. **Give information. Use the ads in 1. Answer B's questions.**

4. **Decide which car you want to buy. Tell B and give your reasons.**

Interactions

Student B

1. **Before you get or give information, use your imagination and complete the car ads.**

    88 BUICK REGAL LTD, pb, ps, pdl, pw, air, _____ dr, am-fm cass, _42_ M, extended wrnty, orig owner, _____ MPG, $_____

    89 FORD TEMPO GLS, _____ M, _____ spd, air, orig owner, blk/gray, must sell. _____ MPG $_____ obo

2. **Give information. Use the ads in 1. Answer A's questions.**

    A: I'm calling about the _'88 Buick Regal_ for sale.

    B: Yes. It's a great buy.

    A: What's the mileage?

    B: _42,000 miles_.

    A: _____?

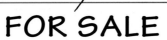

3. **Get information. A put two used car notices on a bulletin board. Call and write the information about A's used cars.**

FOR SALE
'89 Mercury Topaz

FOR SALE
'87 Volkswagen Jetta

	'89 Mercury Topaz	'87 Volkswagen Jetta
Mileage?		
Original owner?		
Miles per gallon?		
Problems?		
Options?		
Price?		
_____?		

4. **Decide which car you want to buy. Tell A and give your reasons.**

Progress Checks ✔

1. **a** ☐ Answer a police officer's questions about a car accident.

What are the people saying?

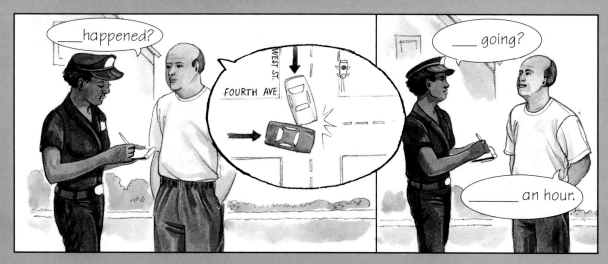

Do it yourself. Talk about the accident in the diagram.

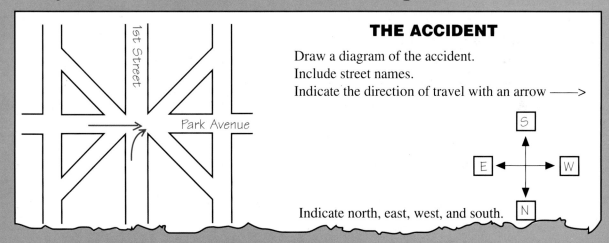

THE ACCIDENT

Draw a diagram of the accident.
Include street names.
Indicate the direction of travel with an arrow ——>

Indicate north, east, west, and south.

2. **d** ☐ Fill out a car accident report.

Look at the diagram in 1. Complete the accident report in 1.

3. **b** ☐ Describe a car in need of repair.

A, tell B about the white car. B, tell A about the gray car.

Progress Checks ✔

4. c ☐ Read used car ads.

89 BUICK SKYLARK	85 VOLVO 440	88 CHEVY SPECTRUM
auto trans, air, pw, pdl, ps, pb, am-fm stereo cass, 37M, 24 mpg, $6300 (209) 885-9436	am-fm ster cass, ps, pw, pdl, pwr seats 29 mpg, 75M, must sell, $2900 (209) 493-1358	air, 4 dr, ps, am-fm cass, silver metallic, 30M, xlnt cond, $3200 obo (209) 537-9302

1.   2.   3.

Write the number of the ad or ads.

1. You want a car with power steering. ____

2. You want a car with air-conditioning. ____

3. You want a car with under 40,000 miles. ____

4. You want a car with an AM/FM cassette. ____

5. You want a car in excellent condition. ____

5. e ☐ Ask and answer questions about a used car.

**A, cover the ads in 4. Ask B about the Buick. B, answer A's questions.
B, cover the ads in 4. Ask A about the Chevy. A, answer B's questions.**

Problem Solving

What's Pete's problem?

What should Pete do?
Now role play.
What kinds of problems have you had driving?

Getting Started

1. **Guess. Where are Marco and Carlos? What are they doing? What are they saying? What's going to happen next?**

2. **What can you hear?**

Conertsations

1. Practice.

Marco: Hi, Carlos. What's up?
Carlos: Are you doing anything Saturday night? *Jokers Are Wild* is opening at the Cinema Six.
Marco: *Jokers Are Wild*? That's supposed to be really funny. But I can't make it until 9:00. I'm taking my mother to the airport.
Carlos: No problem. There's a 10:00 show.
Marco: OK. I'll meet you at the box office at 9:45.
Carlos: Um, wait. I'll meet you at the box office at 9:30. There'll probably be a line.

2. Add two words or phrases with similar meanings.

What's up?	*It's supposed to be*	*funny*
	I hear that it's	

3. Focus on grammar. Review.

Are you	doing anything Saturday night?	I'm	taking my mother to the airport.
Is John	getting tickets to the soccer game?	No, we're	going to the movies on Sunday.

4. Talk about the schedules.

A: Is <u>Manny</u> doing anything this weekend?

B: <u>He's working on Saturday, and he's playing cards on Sunday</u>.

Saturday/Sunday April 24th/April 25th
Saturday Work
Sunday Cards with Carlos and Marco

Manny

Saturday/Sunday April 24th/25th
Saturday Work
Sunday Dinner with Bill

Anda

Saturday/Sunday April 24th/25th
Saturday Clean house
Sunday Zoo

Debra

Saturday/Sunday April 24/25
Saturday Take kids to the park
Sunday Wash car

Li-Wu

Conversations _____

5. Talk about your weekend schedule.

A: Are you doing anything this weekend?

B: No, not really.   OR   <u>I'm going to a baseball game</u>.

6. Practice.

Marco: Did you see *He Rides Again*?
        It was on TV last night.
Carlos: No. What kind of movie was it?
Marco: A western. What kind of movies do you like?
Carlos: Well, I don't like westerns, but I like
        comedies and science-fiction movies.
Marco: Oh, then you should see *Return from Mars*.
        It just came out on video. You'll like it.

a **7. Talk about the movies. Use the conversation in 6 and say what movies you really like. Change partners after each conversation.**

western

love story

science-fiction movie

horror movie

comedy

action/adventure movie

Conversations

8. Practice.

Carlos: What are you doing tomorrow, Marco?
Marco: Well, I'll be at my sister's in the morning. Why?
Carlos: Can I come over and borrow your drill?
Marco: Sure.
Carlos: Oh, good. When will you be home?
Marco: I probably won't be home until noon.
Carlos: OK. I'll call you around 12:00.
Marco: Fine. Gee, it's late. I've got to go.
Carlos: OK. I'll see you tomorrow.

9. Focus on grammar. Review.

I'll be	at my sister's house tomorrow morning.
I won't be	

When will you be home?	Will she be home around 12:00?

10. Talk about your schedule for tomorrow. Use any times.

A: When will you be home tomorrow?

B: _Well, I'll be at work until 5:00. I guess I won't be home until 6:00_.

What about you?

b **11. Talk about leaving. End a conversation politely.**

A: _There's my bus. I've got to go_.

B: _OK. I'll see you tomorrow_.

Paperwork _____

1. **Read the TV schedule. Circle a word you want to learn. Work with your classmates. Find out what it means.**

<table>
<tr><td colspan="8" align="center">**THURSDAY NIGHT**
PRIME-TIME VIEWING GUIDE</td></tr>
<tr><td></td><td>**8:00**</td><td>**8:30**</td><td>**9:00**</td><td>**9:30**</td><td>**10:00**</td><td>**10:30**</td><td>**11:00**</td></tr>
<tr><td>**ABS 4**</td><td colspan="2">Cops and Robbers</td><td>Laugh Track</td><td>Ghostly Tales</td><td colspan="2">Suki Young, P.I.</td><td>Local News</td></tr>
<tr><td>**SBS 6**</td><td colspan="2">Whodunnit?</td><td>Secret Camera</td><td>Oops!</td><td>Sports Legends</td><td>Hot Dogs</td><td>Local News</td></tr>
<tr><td>**PBC 8**</td><td colspan="2">Mother Earth's Children</td><td>Senior City</td><td>Leaping Lizards</td><td colspan="2">Music of the Masters</td><td>This Week in History</td></tr>
<tr><td>**MOVI 14**</td><td colspan="2">He Rides Again! (from 7:00)</td><td colspan="3">Sister Meg and the Bad Egg</td><td>Comedy King</td><td>A Shiver Up His Spine (to 12:30)</td></tr>
</table>

c 2. **Work in pairs. Answer the questions.**

a. What's on at 9:00? <u>Laugh Track</u>

_____

b. What time is *Suki Young, P.I.* on? _____

c. What channel is *This Week in History* on? _____

d. How long is *He Rides Again*? _____

3. **Add questions with your classmates. Then interview three classmates.**

How much television do you watch each week? <u>20 hours</u>

Do you watch TV in English? <u>yes</u>

What's your favorite show? <u>"I Love Lucy" reruns</u>

_____? _____

4. **Pool your information. Then write summary sentences.**

Reading and Writing _____

1. **Work in pairs. You have two minutes. Look at the titles of the movies in 2 and guess what kinds of movies they are. Write your guesses on a separate piece of paper.**

2. **Read the movie reviews. Circle a word you want to learn. Work with your classmates. Find out what it means.**

● ● ● ● ● ● ● ● ● ● ● ● ● ● ● ● ● ● ●

BRIEF MOVIE REVIEWS

G	General Audiences — for all ages
PG	Parental Guidance — some material may be unsuitable for children
PG-13	Parental Guidance — some material may be unsuitable for children under 13
R	Restricted — children under 17 must be accompanied by an adult
NC-17	No Children under 17 — no children under 17 will be admitted

Jokers are Wild—(98 min.) Very funny. Two men in their mid-twenties leave their jobs to drive across the country. They are looking for adventure and freedom. There are lots of laughs along the road and plenty of beautiful scenery. (G)

A Broken Heart—(128 min.) This summer's hottest romance. Filmed in black and white, this movie follows a relationship from its start to its finish. *A Broken Heart* is not your typical boy-meets-girl, boy-loses-girl story. The characters seem very real, and the acting is wonderful—a must see. (R)

The Bug from Planet Mars—(110 min.) A giant insect, brought back to Earth in a satellite, grows to the size of an elephant and frightens a small New England town. This film bores more than it entertains. (PG)

Dial 911—(125 min.) Fine police drama about a young detective trying to find a serial killer before he kills again. Great performances and a well-written script. You will be sitting on the edge of your seat. (PG-13)

Tall in the Saddle—(106 min.) Two young brothers try to find the horse thieves who killed their father. Filmed in the Rocky Mountains, this is a heartwarming story about growing up in the 1890s. (PG)

3. **Read the reviews again. How many of your guesses were correct?**

4. **Work in pairs. Answer these questions about the movies in 2.**

   a. Which movies would you take a 10-year-old child to see?
   b. Which movies are shorter than two hours?
   c. Which movies does the reviewer like?

5. **Work in pairs. Next to each review, write what kind of movie it is. Then compare your answers to your guesses in 1.**

Reading and Writing _____

6. Read the note Carlos left for his roommate, Ben.

7. Imagine that you are going to one of the places below for the evening. Leave a note for someone. Use the note in 6 as an example. Then read your note to your group.

8. Write in your journal. Compare entertainment in the United States and your country.

Listening Plus _____

1. Listen to the contrast. Point.

Time	Place
Time	**Place**
I'll be at the mall at <u>2:00</u>.	I'll be at the <u>mall</u> at 2:00.

Underline the time or place in each sentence.

1. I'll meet you at the theater at 9:00.
2. Ann was at the movies Friday night.
3. You're going to the beach on Sunday?
4. We'll see you at the park at 8:30.
5. We're meeting at Meg's at 8:00.
6. You're leaving for the game at 11:00?

2. Listen. Number the pictures.

Listen again. What do you think the next speaker will say?

3. Call the *CinemaPhone*. You want information about *Terminator 5* and *Batman 6*. Use the keypad. Instead of pushing a button, check (√) it. Fill in the information in the chart.

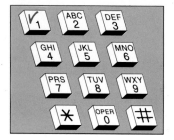

	TERMINATOR 5	**BATMAN 6**
RATING		
MOVIE THEATER LOCATION		
TIMES		

Interactions _____

Student A

1. **Complete your schedule. Leave some free time.**

	Friday	Saturday	Sunday
afternoon			
evening			
night			

2. **You want to go to the movies. You are going to call B. Here are reviews of three movies that are playing at a theater near you. B has the movie schedule.**

Very Funny!—A sweet comedy about a boy who thinks he's a dog. *Very Funny!* is indeed very funny. It'll keep you laughing.—PG

Test of Courage— This year's best action movie. Great car chase scenes. Fine acting.—R

Cave of Fear—A young married couple, lost during a terrible storm, seeks shelter in a haunted cave. Scary! You'll be on the edge of your seat.—NC-17

e 3. **Call B. Use the schedule in 1 and the reviews in 2. Decide together when you are both free and which movie to see. Continue the conversation.**

B: Hello.

A: Hi, _____. This is _____.

Do you want to go to the movies this weekend?

B: Sure. When are you free?

A: _____.

4. **Answer these questions together.**

Which movie are you going to see? _____

What day are you going? _____

What time does the show start? _____

5. **Find out about going to the movies in your partner's country.**

Interactions

Student B

1. **Complete your schedule. Leave some free time.**

	Friday	Saturday	Sunday
afternoon			
evening			
night			

e 2. **A is going to call you about going to the movies. Here is the movie schedule. A has the movie reviews.**

Cinema Route 36 Triplex (209) 584-0894

I   Fri. Sat. Sun. **Test of Courage** (R) 2, 3:50, 5:40, 7:30, 9:30. Mon.–Thurs. 5:10, 7, 9

II Fri. Sat. Sun. **Very Funny!** (PG) 2:10, 4:30, 7:15, 9:45. Mon.–Thurs. 5, 8:30

III Fri. Sat. Sun. **Cave of Fear** (NC-17) 2, 4:10, 6:15, 8:20, 10:20. Mon.–Thurs. 4:50, 7:45

3. **Answer the phone. Use the schedule in 1 and the movie schedule in 2. Decide together when you are both free and which movie to see. Continue the conversation.**

   B: Hello.

   A: Hi, _____. This is _____.

      Do you want to go to the movies this weekend?

   B: Sure. When are you free?

   A: _____.

4. **Answer these questions together.**

   Which movie are you going to see? _____

   What day are you going? _____

   What time does the show start? _____

5. **Find out about going to the movies in your partner's country.**

Progress Checks ✔

1. **c** ☐ Read a TV schedule.

Saturday Night — Prime-Time Schedule							
	8:00	8:30	9:00	9:30	10:00	10:30	11:00
ABS 4	What's Up?	Super Sam	Bet Your Boots	You Don't Say!	I Hate Saturdays!		Local News
SBS 6	Thunder Point		Kung Fu Master	Doc Willis	Hollywood Cops		Local News
PBC 8	Hometown Heroes		Ask the Expert	Comedy Break	Sing for Your Supper		Weekend & Wally
MOVI 14	Near Miss (from 6:30)	Buddies: A Mystery			Search for the Wind		

Answer these questions.

a. What time is *Comedy Break* on? _____ What channel? _____

b. What's on at 10:00? _____

c. What's on at the same time as *Ask the Expert*? _____

_____

2. **a** ☐ Start and maintain a conversation about entertainment.
   b ☐ End a conversation politely.

What are the people saying?

Do it yourself.

Progress Checks ✔

3. **e** ☐ Use a telephone to make routine social plans.

What are the people saying?

Do it yourself.

4. **d** ☐ Get information about entertainment from recorded messages.

Call a movie theater and find out the show times for a movie you want to see. Write the information.

Movie: _____   Times: _____

Problem Solving

What's Martha's problem?

What should Martha do?
Now role play.
What kinds of problems have you had at the movies?

4 Health

Getting Started _____

1. **Guess. Where are Lucy and the nurse? What are they doing? What are they saying? What's going to happen next?**

2. **What can you hear?**

Conversations _____

1. Practice.

Nurse: What's the problem, Mrs. Santana?
Lucy: My daughter has a fever and a rash.
Nurse: Have you given her any medication?
Lucy: Yes, I have. I gave her children's Tylenol, and her fever has gone down, but the rash is still itching a lot.
Nurse: I see. Have you done anything for it?
Lucy: No, I haven't. I didn't know what to do.

2. Focus on grammar.

Have	you	given her any medication?	Yes, I have.
			No, I haven't.
Has	her fever	gone down?	Yes, it has.
			No, it hasn't.

3. Talk about someone's health. Help someone describe a medical problem.

A: What's the problem?

B: My _son_ has _a stomachache_.

A: I see. Have you done anything for it?

B: Yes, I have. _I gave him milk of magnesia_.

OR No, I haven't. I didn't know what to do.

a stomachache
give him milk of magnesia

an ear infection
?

a terrible sunburn
give her a cool bath

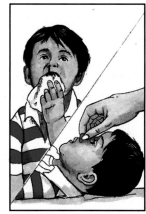

a bad nosebleed
apply pressure

a swollen eyelid
?

Conversations _____

4. Practice.

Nurse: Has Rosie ever had chicken pox?
Lucy: No. She's never had chicken pox.
Nurse: Has she ever had German measles?
Lucy: Yes. She had German measles in 1992.
Nurse: What about the regular measles?
Lucy: No. She had a measles vaccination when she was a baby.
Nurse: That's good. Have a seat. The doctor will be with you soon.

5. Focus on grammar.

| Have you ever had German measles? | Yes. I had German measles | in 1992. last year. |
| | No. I've never had German measles. | |

| I've = I have | she's = she has | he's = he has |

| you've = you have | we've = we have | they've = they have |

b

6. Talk about Rosie's medical history.

A: Has Rosie ever had <u>German measles</u>?

B: <u>Yes. She had German measles in 1992</u>.

Has she ever had <u>the measles</u>?

A: <u>No. She's never had the measles</u>.

7. Talk about your medical history. Use the childhood diseases in 6.

A: Have you ever had <u>chicken pox</u>?

B: <u>Yes. I had chicken pox in 1956</u>.

OR <u>No. I've never had the chicken pox</u>.

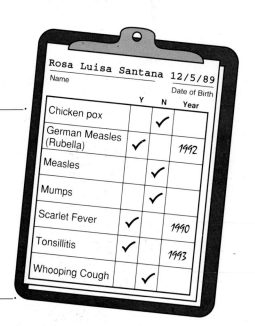

Rosa Luisa Santana 12/5/89
Name   Date of Birth

	Y	N	Year
Chicken pox		✓	
German Measles (Rubella)	✓		1992
Measles		✓	
Mumps		✓	
Scarlet Fever	✓		1990
Tonsillitis	✓		1993
Whooping Cough		✓	

Conversations

8. Practice.

Pharmacist:	Hello, Mrs. Santana. How are you?
Lucy:	OK. But Rosie has a bad case of chicken pox.
Pharmacist:	Chicken pox? Didn't she have chicken pox last year?
Lucy:	No. She had German measles last year.
Pharmacist:	Oh, right. Do you need something for the itch?
Lucy:	Yes, a lotion and an antihistamine. Rosie has never taken an antihistamine. Are there any side effects?
Pharmacist:	It may cause drowsiness or nervousness. And you're not supposed to drink alcohol while you're taking it.
Lucy:	I'm sorry?
Pharmacist:	You shouldn't drink alcohol when you're taking an antihistamine. But that's no problem for Rosie!

9. Add two words or phrases with similar meanings.

may	*you're not supposed to*	*I'm sorry?*
could		
_____	_____	_____
_____	_____	_____

10. Talk about the medicine. Rephrase the instructions.

A: Remember. You're <u>not supposed to drink alcoholic</u> <u>beverages when you're taking this medication</u>.

B: I'm sorry?

A: <u>Don't drink alcohol when you're taking this</u>.

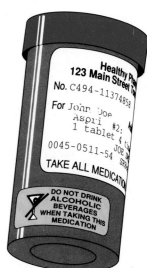

 TAKE WITH **FOOD**

NOT TO BE TAKEN BY **MOUTH**

DO **NOT** TAKE WITH **ASPIRIN**

DO NOT TAKE WITH **DAIRY PRODUCTS**

 TAKE **MEDICATION** ON AN **EMPTY STOMACH**

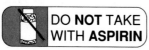 TAKE WITH PLENTY OF **WATER**

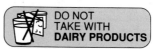 DRINK **ORANGE JUICE** OR EAT A **BANANA DAILY** WHILE TAKING THIS MEDICATION

Paperwork _____

1. **Read the application for health insurance. Circle a word you want to learn. Work with your classmates. Find out what it means.**

APPLICATION FOR MUTUAL GROUP MEDICAL INSURANCE

Name _____ Occupation _____
        First   Middle   Last

Soc. Sec. # _____

Billing Address _____
                Street   City   State   ZIP

Date of Birth _____ Sex _____ Height ___ft. ___in. Weight _____lbs.

1. If you are also applying for dependent coverage, complete below:

   Spouse's First Name_____ Date of Birth_____ Height_____ Weight_____

First Name of Child	Date of Birth	First Name of Child	Date of Birth
_____	_____	_____	_____
_____	_____	_____	_____
_____	_____	_____	_____

2. During the past 5 years, have you or any of your dependents in 1:
   a) Seen a physician?   ☐ YES ☐ NO
   b) Been in a hospital or had an operation?   ☐ YES ☐ NO

3. Are you or any of your dependents in 1 taking medication?   ☐ YES ☐ NO

4. Do you or any of your dependents in 1 have any physical or mental health problems?   ☐ YES ☐ NO

5. Have you or any of your dependents in 1 ever had:
   a) AIDS, heart disease, stroke, cancer, diabetes, or epilepsy?   ☐ YES ☐ NO
   b) High blood pressure, arthritis, back trouble, or an alcohol or drug habit?   ☐ YES ☐ NO
   c) A disease of the circulatory, digestive, urinary, respiratory, or reproductive systems?   ☐ YES ☐ NO

---

e   2. **Fill in the application for yourself.**

3. **Add questions with your classmates. Then interview three classmates.**

What kind of health insurance do you have?   Blue Cross and Blue Shield

Who pays for your health insurance?   my employer

Where do you go for medical help?   Westside Clinic

_____?

4. **Pool your information. Then write summary sentences.**

Reading and Writing

1. Skim the information from the cold medicine box in 2. In which section will you find information about the amount of medicine to take? The reasons for taking this medicine? The side effects this medicine can cause?

2. Read the information from the cold medicine box. Circle a word you want to learn. Work with your classmates. Find out what it means.

=COLD ARREST= MEDICATION

DO NOT USE IF CARTON IS OPENED. EACH CAPLET IS SAFETY SEALED. DO NOT USE IF BLISTER OR FOIL IS BROKEN.

Keep this and all drugs out of reach of children. In case of accidental overdose, contact a physician or Poison Control Center immediately.

INDICATIONS: For the temporary relief of runny nose, sneezing, itching of the nose or throat, itchy watery eyes due to allergies and common colds.
DIRECTIONS: ADULTS: 1 or 2 caplets every 4 to 6 hours, not to exceed 12 caplets in 24 hours, or as directed by a physician.

CHILDREN 6 TO 12 YEARS: 1 caplet every 4 to 6 hours, not to exceed 6 caplets in 24 hours for five days, or as directed by a physician.
CHILDREN UNDER 6: consult a physician for the correct dosage.
WARNINGS: May cause nervousness especially in children. May cause drowsiness. Alcohol may increase the drowsiness effect. Avoid alcoholic beverages while taking this product. Use caution when driving a motor vehicle or operating machinery. As with any drug, if you are pregnant or nursing a baby, ask your doctor before using this product. Do not take this product if you have heart disease, high blood pressure, thyroid disease, diabetes, or asthma.

3. Read the information again. How many of your answers in 1 were correct?

4. Work in pairs. All of these people have bad colds. Which of them can take the medicine in 2 without consulting their doctors? Circle the letters, and write their correct dosages on the lines to the right.

   a. a 50-year-old woman _____

   b. a 4-year-old boy _____

   c. a 10-year-old girl with asthma _____

   d. a 12-year-old boy with allergies _____

   e. a 25-year-old pregnant woman _____

   f. a 40-year-old school bus driver _____

Reading and Writing _____

5. **Read Debra's record of her son's immunizations.**

Andy		
DATE	AGE	IMMUNIZATIONS
4-6-83	2 mos.	Diptheria, pertussis, and tetanus (DPT), polio
6-7-83	4 mos.	DPT, polio
8-10-83	6 mos.	DPT
3-9-84	13 mos.	Measles, mumps, German measles
8-7-84	18 mos.	DPT, polio

6. **Read Debra's own medical history.**

Debra		
DATE	REASON FOR MEDICAL ATTENTION	DOCTOR
1960	Mumps	Dr. Williams
1966	Tonsillectomy	Dr. Scalia
1979	Broken leg from car accident	Dr. Gonzalez
2-4-83	Gave birth to Andy	Dr. Levine
12-11-91	Pneumonia-Bridgeton General	Dr. Newman

7. **Start a medical record book of your own for yourself or a family member. Show it to your partner if you like.**

8. **Write in your journal. Compare health care in the United States and in your country.**

Listening Plus _____

1. Listen to the contrast. Point.

Thing	**Time**
She had <u>German measles</u> last year.	She had German measles <u>last year</u>.

Underline the thing or time in each sentence.

1. She had an earache last night.
2. She had German measles last month.
3. I have an appointment tomorrow.
4. He had a cold last month.
5. I took my pills at 10:00.
6. I had my appendix removed last year.

2. Listen. Number the pictures.

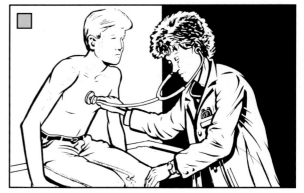

Listen again. What do you think the next speaker will say?

3. Dr. Carson is returning calls. Write down what is wrong with the patient and what the patient should and shouldn't do.

chicken pox	

Interactions

Student A

1. **Take turns getting and giving information. Complete the puzzle.**

A: What's _2 Across_?

B: It's _very, very bad_.

A: _Terrible_?

B: That's right.

A: How do you spell that?

B: T-E-R-R-I-B-L-E. What's _1 Down_?

A: It's _how you feel when you're not happy_.

B: _Bad_?

A: No. _Another word for unhappy_.

	¹S		²T	E	R	R	I	³B	L	E			⁴L	E	F	⁵T
⁶	A							A								
	D			⁷S	U	N	B	U	R	⁸N						
⁹							Y			O						
¹⁰N	I	¹¹N	E			¹²M				S						
		O				U		¹³P	R	E	G	N	A	¹⁴N	T	
						M				B				U		
¹⁵		¹⁶I				P				L		¹⁷		R		
		T				S			¹⁸	E				S		
		C		¹⁹		²⁰		²¹B		E				E		
	²²H	O	S	P	I	T	A	L		²³D		²⁴		S		
								D								

2. **Find out about going to the doctor in your partner's country.**

Interactions

Student B

1. **Take turns getting and giving information. Complete the puzzle.**

A: What's _2 Across_?

B: It's _very very bad_.

A: _Terrible_?

B: That's right.

A: How do you spell that?

B: T-E-R-R-I-B-L-E. What's _1 Down_?

A: It's _how you feel when you're not happy_.

B: _Bad_?

A: No. _Another word for unhappy_.

2. **Find out about going to the doctor in your partner's country.**

Progress Checks ✔

1. **e** ☐ Fill in a group medical insurance application form.

Complete the application.

Date of Birth _____ Sex _____ · Height ___ft. ___in. Weight _____lbs.

1. **If you are also applying for dependent coverage, complete below:**

Spouse's First Name _____ Date of Birth_____ Height_____ Weight_____

First Name of Child	Date of Birth	First Name of Child	Date of Birth

2. **During the past 5 years, have you or any of your dependents in 1:**
   a) Seen a physician? Yes ___ No ___
   b) Been in a hospital or had an operation? Yes ___ No ___

3. **Are you or any of your dependents in 1 taking medication?** Yes ___ No ___

4. **Do you or any of your dependents in 1 have any physical or mental health problems?** Yes ___ No ___

5. **Have you or any of your dependents in 1 ever had:**
   a) AIDS, heart disease, stroke, cancer, diabetes, or epilepsy? Yes ___ No ___
   b) High blood pressure, arthritis, back trouble, or an alcohol or drug habit? Yes ___ No ___
   c) A disease of the circulatory, digestive, urinary, respiratory, or reproductive systems? Yes ___ No ___

2. **c** ☐ Read warning labels on medicine.
   d ☐ Rephrase instructions.

What are the people saying?

Do it yourself. Choose one of the labels above.

Progress Checks

3. **a** ☐ Explain your own or someone else's medical problem.
  b ☐ Give information about your own or someone else's childhood diseases.

What are the people saying?

Do it yourself.

Problem Solving

What's Jeff's problem?

What should Sue do?
Now role play.
What kinds of medical emergencies have you had?

5 Finding a Job

Getting Started

1. **Guess. Where are Chen and the receptionist? What are they doing? What are they saying? What's going to happen next?**

2. **What can you hear?**

Conversations _____

1. Practice.

Chen: I'm calling about the sales manager position in *The Sun Times*.
Receptionist: Oh, yes. Have you had any experience?
Chen: Well, I've been a salesperson for three years.
      I've sold electronic equipment, and I've done inventory control.
Receptionist: Can you come to our agency to fill in an application?
Chen: Sure. Can you give me directions, please?

2. Focus on grammar.

He's	**had**	a lot of experience.
	installed	heaters.
	repaired	sinks.

He's = He has

answer	answered	**answered**
help	helped	**helped**
type	typed	**typed**
use	used	**used**

do	did	**done**
make	made	**made**
sell	sold	**sold**
take	took	**taken**

3. Talk about the people. Use the verbs in 2.

A: Has ___Chen___ had any experience as a ___sales manager___?

B: Well, ___he's___ been ___a salesperson___ for ___three years___.
 ___He's sold electronic equipment, and he's done inventory control___.

Li-Wu Chen sales manager salesperson— 3 yrs. electronic equipment inventory control	Barbara Gates cook cafeteria worker— 5 yrs. orders sandwiches	Cathy Gibson bank teller cashier—8 yrs. cash register customers	Jim Doyle secretary administrative assistant—2 yrs. phones letters and memos

Conversations _____

4. Practice.

Ms. Silver: And how long have you been
a salesperson?
Chen: For several years. Since 1990.
Ms. Silver: And how many jobs have you had?
Chen: Just the one at Logan's.
Ms. Silver: I see. So you've never been a
sales manager?
Chen: No, but I've taken business courses
at Bridgeton Community College.

5. Focus on grammar.

How long have you been a salesperson?	For	four years. six months.
	Since	1990. March.

6. Talk about the people.

A: What kind of work does <u>Chen</u> do?

B: <u>He's a salesperson</u> .

A: How long has <u>he</u> been <u>a salesperson</u> ?

B: <u>For three years</u>. OR <u>Since 1990</u> .

Name *Li-Wu Chen*

Dates	Employer	Position
2/90-Pres.	Logan's	Salesperson

Name *Larry Kramer*

Dates	Employer	Position
1/85-Pres	Safe-Key	Locksmith

Name *Nancy Dobbs*

Dates	Employer	Position
2/89-Pres.	Farrel & Brown	Accountant

Name *Tim Harmon*

Dates	Employer	Position
8/90-Pres.	P.S. 152	Security Guard
5/89-7/90	R&N Dept. Store	Security Guard.

Name *Dorothy Parker*

Dates	Employer	Position
9/91-pres.	General Hospital	Nurse's Aide
7/90-8/91	Hillcrest Home	Nurse's Aide

7. Talk about yourself. Use the conversation in 6. Begin, *What kind of*
work do you do?

Conversations _____

8. Practice.

Chen:	Hello. This is Li-Wu Chen. I applied for the sales manager position at Electronics Plus last week.
Receptionist:	Oh, yes, Mr. Chen. How are you?
Chen:	Fine, thanks. Uh… I was wondering… Have they reviewed my application?
Receptionist:	Yes, they have. As a matter of fact, I'm glad you called. We tried to reach you earlier.
Chen:	I'm sorry. I was out.
Receptionist:	They're interested in your application. Would you be available for an interview on Monday or Tuesday?
Chen:	Sure.

9. Add two words or phrases with similar meanings.

I was wondering	*as a matter of fact*	*reach*
	in fact	

10. Talk about a job. Call about your application for one of the jobs below.

A: Hello. This is _____.

I applied for the job as a _____ last week.

B: Oh, yes, _____.

A: I was wondering… Have you reviewed my application?

B: _Yes, we have. Would you be available for an interview_ ?

OR _No, we haven't. Could you call back later this week_ ?

A: Sure.

Paperwork _____

1. **Read the employment ads. Circle a word you want to learn. Work with your classmates. Find out what it means.**

Office Worker
Top Bridgeton company seeks F/T office worker w/2—5 yrs exp. Excel bnfts. 55 wpm typg reqd. Call Andrea Klar 209-569-3541

Experienced Cooks
PT pos for Westside restaurant serving fine French cuisine. Must have 2 yrs cooking exp. Fax resume to (209) 347-1301

Painter/Mechanic
Needed for Bridgeton ofc complex. Gd oppty. Send resume to: Property Manager, P.O. Box 913, Bridgeton, CA 93204. No phone calls, please.

Truck Driver
2 yrs min exp. Salary range $10 and up. Drug testing reqd. Send resume to S. Lauter Corp., 112 5th Ave., Bridgeton 93206.

Warehouseperson
Lighting co has an immed opening for qualif indiv to receive, stock, & send shipments. High school grad only. (209) 342-8146

Telemarketing-High Comms
Credit card co seeks exp'd telephone sales rep. Temp pos. Call Denise Franco. (209) 743-1287

b

2. **Work in pairs. Write the abbreviations from 1 for these words.**

1. benefits bnfts
2. commissions _____
3. company _____
4. corporation _____
5. excellent _____
6. experience _____
7. experienced _____
8. full-time _____

9. good _____
10. immediate _____
11. individual _____
12. minimum _____
13. office _____
14. opportunity _____
15. part-time _____
16. position _____

17. qualified _____
18. representative _____
19. required _____
20. temporary _____
21. typing _____
22. with _____
23. words per minute _____
24. years _____

3. **Add questions with your classmates. Then interview three classmates.**

Have you ever found a job through the newspaper? _Yes. The job I have now._

How have you looked for a job? _Newspaper ads, Job Service, counselor_

Has it been easy or difficult to find a job in the U.S.? Why? _Difficult. I don't have a car._

_____? _____

4. **Pool your information. Then write summary sentences.**

Reading and Writing _____

1. **Work in pairs. With your books closed, write three kinds of information you think Chen included in his resume.**

2. **Read Chen's resume. Circle a word you want to learn. Work with your classmates. Find out what it means.**

Li-Wu Chen
806 Union Avenue, Bridgeton, CA 93205, (209) 438-9218

OBJECTIVE   A challenging position in sales management

EXPERIENCE
2/90 – Present   **Logan's Department Store. Bridgeton, CA**
                  Salesperson, Electronics Department
                  Sell TVs, VCRs, camcorders, stereo systems, and
                  other home entertainment equipment; handle
                  customer service desk and returns; deal
                  effectively with the public; responsible for
                  inventory control

9/79 – 5/89   **Zen Ai City Hospital. Taipei, Taiwan**
                  Paramedic

EDUCATION
9/92 – Present   Bridgeton Community College, Bridgeton, CA
                  Completed 6 credits: Accounting I and II

9/91 – Present   Westside Community Adult School, Bridgeton, CA
                  English classes

1975 – 1979   Cheng Kung Senior High School, Taiwan

REFERENCES   Available upon request

---

3. **Read the resume again. How many of your answers in 1 were correct?**

C 4. **Write a resume for yourself. Show it to your partner.**

Reading and Writing _____

5. **Chen is replying to an ad in the paper for a sales manager trainee. Read his letter. Circle a word you want to learn. Work with your classmates. Find out what it means.**

806 Union Avenue
Bridgeton, CA 93205

January 28, 1994

Personnel Manager
Broadway Electronics
120 Broadway
Bridgeton, CA 93201

Dear Personnel Manager:

I am responding to your ad for a Sales Manager-Trainee in
the Bridgeton Sun Times of Sunday, January 27, 1994.

I have enclosed a copy of my resume, and I hope to have an
opportunity to talk to you about my background and skills.

I will call you next week to arrange an appointment, if
possible.

Sincerely yours,

Li-Wu Chen

Li-Wu Chen

Enclosure

6. **Complete the ad. Use a job you would like.**

THE DAILY GAZETTE, SUNDAY, MARCH 21, 1996

_____ needed.
Excel salary and bnfts.
Send resume to Personnel
Director, ABC Company,
P. O. Box 213, _____
_____

d | 7. **Write a cover letter to the company in the ad in 6. Show it to your partner.**

8. **Write in your journal. Compare job-hunting in the United States and in your country.**

Listening Plus

1. Listen to the contrast. Point.

Choice	**Yes/No**
Can you come Monday or Tuesday?	Can you come Monday or Tuesday?

Write *C* for *Choice* or *Y/N* for *Yes/No*.

1. Should I speak to Bob or John? __
2. Do you type or use a computer? __
3. Can you come at 9:00 or 10:00? __
4. Do you need a pen or a pencil? __
5. Do you have a degree or experience? __
6. Should I call or send a resume? __

2. Listen. Number the pictures.

Listen again. What do you think the next speaker will say?

3. You're getting directions over the phone to Person Power, an employment agency. Write the directions. Then trace the route on the map.

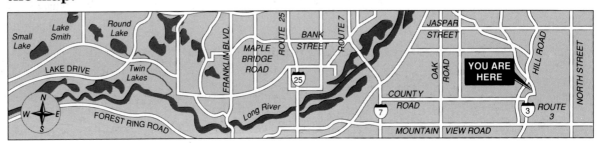

Interactions

Student A

e 1. **Get information. Choose one of the office jobs below. Read the list of questions. Call B about the job. Continue the conversation and take notes. Then check your notes with B.**

A: Hello. My name is _____.

I'm calling about the job as a _____.

Is it still available?

B: Yes, it is.

A: OK. I have a few other questions.

_____?

■ **New Office Now Hiring** ■	
Positions Available	Available? Yes
• Office Manager	Full-time?
• Receptionist	Interview?
(209) 674-1800, ext. 38	Resume?
	Where?
	When?

2. **Give information. Answer B's questions. Use the information from the note and the ads.**

FROM THE DESK OF DAVID WADE

Re: The Cook Position

Tell applicants to send their resumes. We'll call them in about two weeks to set up interviews. Thanks.

COOK
P/T, Tu–Sa, 5 pm–10 pm
Bridgeton's newest downtown restaurant has immed opening for a cook. Send resume to Marbles, 243 Union Ave, Bridgeton, 93201.
Call (209) 712-0094

FROM THE DESK OF DAVID WADE

Re: The Manager Position

Please schedule interviews for next Tuesday and Wednesday. Tell applicants to bring their resumes. Thanks.

RESTAURANT MANAGER F/T
Bridgeton's newest downtown restaurant needs a manager to manage staff & deal w/customers.
Marbles, 243 Union Ave, Bridgeton, 93201.
Call (209) 712-0094

3. **Find out about your partner's job in his or her country.**

Interactions

Student B

1. Give information. Answer A's questions. Use the information from the note and the ads.

FROM THE DESK OF
LAURA MARTINEZ

Re: The Receptionist Position

We will interview applicants next Thursday and Friday.

They will have to fill out applications before their interviews, so they should get here 15 minutes early. Thanks.

RECEPTIONIST
P/T, M-F 8 am - 12 pm
Front desk, busy phone and fax.
Excel salary & bnfts.
R&K Industries Corp.,
1905 12th Ave.,
Bridgeton 93202,
(209) 674-1800 ext 38.

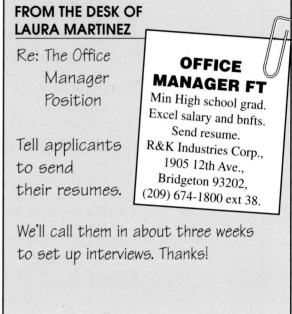

FROM THE DESK OF
LAURA MARTINEZ

Re: The Office Manager Position

Tell applicants to send their resumes.

We'll call them in about three weeks to set up interviews. Thanks!

OFFICE MANAGER FT
Min High school grad.
Excel salary and bnfts.
Send resume.
R&K Industries Corp.,
1905 12th Ave.,
Bridgeton 93202,
(209) 674-1800 ext 38.

e

2. Get information. Choose one of the restaurant jobs below. Read the list of questions. Call A about the job. Continue the conversation and take notes. Then check your notes with A.

A: Hello. My name is _____.

I'm calling about the job as a _____.

Is it still available?

B: Yes, it is.

A: OK. I have a few other questions.

_____?

NEW RESTAURANT NOW HIRING
Positions available
- Manager
- Cook
(209) 712-0094

Available?   Yes
Full-time?
Interview?
Resume?
Where?
When?

3. Find out about your partner's job in his or her country.

Progress Checks ✔

1. **b** ☐ Read employment ads.
   c ☐ Write a basic resume.
   d ☐ Write a cover letter when applying for a job.

   Bring in an employment ad for a job you'd like. Write a cover letter for it, and attach your resume.

2. **e** ☐ Use a telephone to inquire about advertised job openings.

   What are the people saying?

_____ as a secretary.
_____?

Do it yourself.

A, call B about one of the jobs below. B, answer A's questions. Use your imagination.

Secretary Type 55 WPM, file, answer phones, open mail. Min 2 yrs. exp. Excel salary and bnfts. Send resume to R & K Industries Corp., 1905 12th Ave, Bridgeton 93203. (209) 674-1800 ext 38	**Maintenance Manager** Olympia Park needs maintenance person exp'd in plumbing, carpentry, and electrical work. Send resume to Shaw Properties, 1128 Lincoln Ave., Bridgeton 93205. (209) 329-1478 **SALESPERSONS** The Sock It To Me Shop needs exp'd sales staff for its new downtown store. Send resume to 10458 Harrison St., Bridgeton 93202. Attn: Joe or call (209) 842-9304	■ ■ ■ ■ ■ ■ ■ ■ ■ ■ **SERVERS** ■ ■ ■ ■ ■ ■ ■ ■ ■ Bridgeton's newest downtown restaurant seeks mature, responsible servers. Lunch and/or dinner. 1 yr. exp. Send resume to Marbles, 243 Union Ave, Bridgeton 93201. Call (209) 712-0094

Progress Checks ✔

3. **a** ☐   Make a follow-up phone call about a job application.

What are the people saying?

Do it yourself.

A, give B the cover letter and resume from 1. Call B to follow-up about the job.

Problem Solving

What's Mrs. Green's Problem?

How old are you, Mrs. Green?

What should Mrs. Green do?
Now role play.
What kinds of problems have you had on job interviews?

6 Food

Getting Started

1. **Guess. Where are Marco, Lucy, and the waitress? What are they doing? What are they saying? What's going to happen next?**

2. **What can you hear?**

Conventions _____

1. Practice.

Waitress: Hello. Has anyone taken your order yet?
Marco: No, not yet. What are you going to have, Lucy?
Lucy: I don't know. I'm not very hungry.
Marco: How come?
Lucy: I've already eaten. I had a sandwich before class. Let's see....
Maybe I'll get a dessert. The chocolate cake sounds good.
Waitress: OK. One chocolate cake. Would you like coffee or tea?
Lucy: Yes. Coffee, please. Decaf.
Waitress: OK. And what can I get for you, sir?

2. Focus on grammar.

Have they eaten **yet**?	She's **already** eaten.	She ate at 6:00.
	He hasn't eaten **yet**.	He **just** ordered.

3. Talk about the people in the restaurant. Use these verbs:

pay   order   get menus   ask for the check   eat dessert   have drinks

A: <u>Have the people at table 1 gotten menus yet</u>?

B: <u>Yes. They've already ordered</u>. Have the people at <u>table 4 paid yet</u>?

A: <u>No, they haven't paid yet. They just asked for the check</u>.

Conversations _____

4. Invite 5 classmates out to eat.

    A: Would you like to get something to eat after class?

    B: That's a good idea. I haven't had <u>lunch</u> yet.

        OR Thanks, but I've already had <u>lunch.</u> . Maybe some other time.

5. Practice.

Lucy:	How's your chicken, Marco?
Marco:	Pretty good. Would you like to try some?
Lucy:	Oh, no. Thanks.
Marco:	Don't you like fried chicken?
Lucy:	It's OK, as long as it's not too greasy.
Marco:	Yeah. I know what you mean. By the way, how did you find class tonight?
Lucy:	It was tough. What did you think?

6. Add two words or phrases with similar meanings.

I know what you mean.	***How did you find…?***	***tough***
<u>I understand how you feel.</u>	_____	_____
_____	_____	_____

7. Talk about the food. Then use *By the way* to change the topic and continue the conversation.

    A: Do you like <u>fried chicken</u>?

    B: No. I don't eat <u>fried foods</u>.

        OR I don't know. I've never tried <u>it</u>.

        OR Yes, I like <u>it</u> a lot.

        OR Yes, as long as <u>it's</u> not too <u>salty</u>.

    A: By the way, _____.

salty

rare

hot

greasy

rich

Conversations

8. Practice.

Marco: I had a really nice time, Lucy.

Lucy: Me too. Uhm…it's getting late.
I should call home.

Marco: OK. I'll wait for you.

Lucy: Excuse me. Can you tell me where
the phone is?

Cashier: Sorry. We don't have one, but there are
some on the other side of the mall,
next to the exit by Jackson's.

Lucy: The exit near Jackson's? Thanks.

9. Focus on grammar.

Where is the phone?	Can you tell me	where the phone is?
What are your specials?		what your specials are?

10. Ask for information.

A: Excuse me. Can you tell me <u>where the phone is</u> ?

B: <u>Sure. It's near the door</u> .

A: <u>Near the door</u>? Thanks.

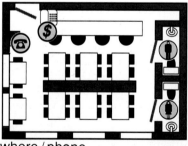

where / phone

Today's Specials	
Meat Loaf	4.95
Fish 'n Chips	5.95
Chili	3.95
Apple Pie	1.50
Rice Pudding	1.25

what / desserts

From the Sandwich Maker	
Ham and Swiss	2.59
Egg Salad	1.89
Turkey Breast	2.89
Tuna	2.29
Roast Beef	2.99

how much / tuna sandwich

Soup of the Day
Mon - Vegetable
Tues - Chicken
Wed - Tomato
Thurs - Onion
Fri - Clam Chowder

what / soup of the day

Side Dishes	
Cole Slaw	.59
Potato Salad	.69
French Fries	.99
Onion Rings	1.19
Green Salad	1.29

how much / french fries

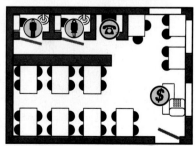

where / restrooms

Paperwork

1. **Read the food labels. Circle a word you want to learn. Work with your classmates. Find out what it means.**

■ LENTIL PILAF MIX ■

Bring 2 cups water and 2 to 3 tablespoons oil to a boil. Stir in lentils, rice, and contents of "Spice Sack." Cover, simmer 35 to 40 minutes or until lentils are tender and water is absorbed. Fluff lentil pilaf lightly with fork before serving. Makes 3 cups.

Hot Wheat Cereal

In saucepan, combine 1 1/2 cups water and 1/2 cup cereal. Heat to a rapid boil, stirring occasionally. Cook 4 to 5 minutes over moderate heat or to desired consistency, stirring occasionally. Remove from heat; cover until ready to serve. Stir before serving.

---

b 2. **Work in pairs. Follow the directions in 1. Number the steps in order.**

3. **Add questions with your classmates. Then interview three classmates.**

Who does the cooking in your house? _I do._

Do you ever eat out? How often? _Yes, about once every two weeks._

What's your favorite American food? _pizza_

_____? _____

4. **Pool your information. Then write summary sentences.**

Unit 6

Reading and Writing

1. Work in pairs. You have one minute. Look at the menu. Do they serve spaghetti? turkey salad? cherry pie? decaffeinated coffee? spinach?

2. Read the menu. Circle a word you want to learn. Work with your classmates. Find out what it means.

Family Restaurant

Famous Burgers
Charbroiled Juicy Burger	$4.45
Cheesburger	4.75
Bacon Cheeseburger	4.99

Sandwiches
Tuna Salad	$4.25
Chicken Salad	4.25
Grilled Cheese	2.99
Ham and Swiss	4.85
Turkey Breast	4.25

Salads
House Salad	$3.25
Chunk Tuna Salad	5.15
Chef Salad	5.29
Grilled Chicken Salad	5.55

Beef
Sirloin Steak	$6.55
Meat Loaf	6.75
Roast Beef	6.50

Desserts
Fresh Baked Apple Pie	$1.79
a la mode	2.25
New York Cheesecake	1.99
Decadent Hot Fudge Cake	2.45
Sundaes	2.25
Ice Cream	
1 scoop	.85
2 scoops	1.25

Chicken
Grilled Chicken	$6.55
BBQ Chicken	6.55
Fried Chicken	5.95

Seafood
Golden Fried Shrimp	$7.35
Fish & Chips	4.99
Broiled Filet of Sole	6.95

Pasta
Spaghetti and Meatballs	$5.19
Linguine and Marinara Sauce	4.35
Lasagna	4.99

Soups and Sides
Fresh Vegetables				$1.25
Carrots, Peas, Broccoli, Green Beans				
Zesty Chili	Cup	1.99	Bowl	2.99
Golden Brown French Fries				1.09
Cole Slaw				1.19
Soup	Cup	.99	Bowl	1.49
Chicken, Vegetable, Soup of the Day				

Beverages
Soft Drinks	reg.	.89	lg.	.99
Cola, Root Beer, Lemon-Lime				
Juice	reg.	.99	lg.	1.49
Orange, Apple, Tomato				
Hot Tea	.60	Iced Tea		.99
Coffee	.60	Hot Chocolate		.89
Decaf	.70	Milk		.99

3. Read the menu again. How many of your answers in 1 were correct?

Reading and Writing

4. **Work with a partner. Look at the menu and the restaurant check. Find the mistakes in the check and circle them. Compare your answers with another pair. Note: Do not change the tax. The tax is correct.**

GUEST CHECK

1 Cup Vegetable Soup		99
1 Tuna Sandwich	5	15
1 Grilled Chicken Salad	5	55
2 Regular Colas		99
1 Apple pie w/vanilla ice cream	2	25
1 Hot Chocolate		89
1 Decaf		70
Subtotal	16	52
Tax	1	35
Total	17	87

PLEASE PAY CASHIER

5. **Student A, you're a customer. Look at the menu and order a meal. Student B, you're the server. Take the order. Look at the menu and write up the check. Figure out the total and give A the check. A, make sure it is correct.**

6. **Tips are usually 15% – 20% of the total before tax, if service is good. A, how much do you want to leave your server for a tip?**

7. **Write in your journal. Compare food in the United States and in your country.**

Listening Plus _____

<cassette> **1.** **Listen to the contrast. Point.**

<table>
<tr><th align="center">Choice</th><th align="center">Yes/No</th></tr>
<tr><td>Would you like coffee or tea?</td><td>Would you like coffee or tea?</td></tr>
</table>

Write *C* for *Choice* or *Y/N* for *Yes/No*.

1. Would you like milk or lemon? ___   2. Do you want Mexican or Thai food? ___

3. Did Janice or Alan make it? ___   4. Will you get the cake or the sundae? ___

5. Should I make chicken or fish? ___   6. Do you want to go today or Friday? ___

2. **Listen. Number the pictures.**

Listen again. What do you think the next speaker will say?

3. **Customers are calling Luigi's Pizzeria. Take their orders and figure out their checks. Medium pies are $7.50; large pies, $9.50; each topping is $1.00.**

<table>
<tr><td colspan="3">Name:_____</td></tr>
<tr><td colspan="3">Address:_____</td></tr>
<tr><td colspan="3">Pick-up Time:_____ Delivery Time:_____</td></tr>
<tr><td colspan="3">Phone #:_____</td></tr>
<tr><td>Pizza: ☐ med ☐ lg</td><td>☐ Anchovies</td><td>☐ Mushrooms</td></tr>
<tr><td rowspan="5">**Total:**</td><td>☐ Black Olives</td><td>☐ Onions</td></tr>
<tr><td>☐ Broccoli</td><td>☐ Pepperoni</td></tr>
<tr><td>☐ Double Cheese</td><td>☐ Peppers</td></tr>
<tr><td>☐ Fresh Garlic</td><td>☐ Spinach</td></tr>
</table>

<table>
<tr><td colspan="3">Name:_____</td></tr>
<tr><td colspan="3">Address:_____</td></tr>
<tr><td colspan="3">Pick-up Time:_____ Delivery Time:_____</td></tr>
<tr><td colspan="3">Phone #:_____</td></tr>
<tr><td>Pizza: ☐ med ☐ lg</td><td>☐ Anchovies</td><td>☐ Mushrooms</td></tr>
<tr><td rowspan="5">**Total:**</td><td>☐ Black Olives</td><td>☐ Onions</td></tr>
<tr><td>☐ Broccoli</td><td>☐ Pepperoni</td></tr>
<tr><td>☐ Double Cheese</td><td>☐ Peppers</td></tr>
<tr><td>☐ Fresh Garlic</td><td>☐ Spinach</td></tr>
</table>

Interactions

Student A

1. **Get information. You're at the mall information booth. Ask for the locations of six places you want to go to that aren't numbered on your directory. Then write the names of the stores on your map.**

    A: Excuse me. Can you tell me where <u>Mrs. Stone's Cookies</u> is?

    B: Yes. <u>Go straight down the main corridor toward Sands. It's on the left, just past the elevator</u>.

    A: <u>On the left, just past the elevator</u>?

    B: That's right. <u>And just before the escalator</u>.

    B: Thanks.

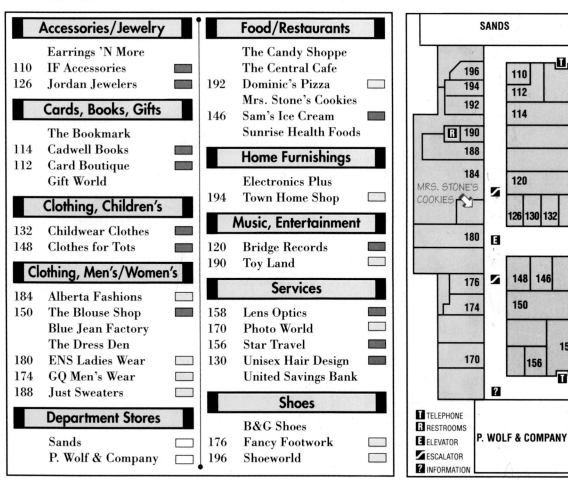

Accessories/Jewelry	
	Earrings 'N More
110	IF Accessories
126	Jordan Jewelers

Cards, Books, Gifts	
	The Bookmark
114	Cadwell Books
112	Card Boutique
	Gift World

Clothing, Children's	
132	Childwear Clothes
148	Clothes for Tots

Clothing, Men's/Women's	
184	Alberta Fashions
150	The Blouse Shop
	Blue Jean Factory
	The Dress Den
180	ENS Ladies Wear
174	GQ Men's Wear
188	Just Sweaters

Department Stores	
	Sands
	P. Wolf & Company

Food/Restaurants	
	The Candy Shoppe
	The Central Cafe
192	Dominic's Pizza
	Mrs. Stone's Cookies
146	Sam's Ice Cream
	Sunrise Health Foods

Home Furnishings	
	Electronics Plus
194	Town Home Shop

Music, Entertainment	
120	Bridge Records
190	Toy Land

Services	
158	Lens Optics
170	Photo World
156	Star Travel
130	Unisex Hair Design
	United Savings Bank

Shoes	
	B&G Shoes
176	Fancy Footwork
196	Shoeworld

SANDS

T TELEPHONE
R RESTROOMS
E ELEVATOR
Z ESCALATOR
? INFORMATION

P. WOLF & COMPANY

2. **Give information. You work at the mall information booth. Answer B's questions. Write the store name in the correct location on your map.**

3. **Find out about places to shop and eat in your partner's country.**

Interactions

Student B

d   1. Give information. You work at the mall information booth. Answer A's questions. Write the store name in the correct location on your map.

A: Excuse me. Can you tell me where <u>Mrs. Stone's Cookies</u> is?

B: Yes. ___<u>Go straight down the main corridor toward Sands. It's on the</u>___
   ___<u>left, just past the elevator</u>___.

A: ___<u>On the left, just past the elevator</u>___?

B: That's right. ___<u>And just before the escalator</u>___.

B: Thanks.

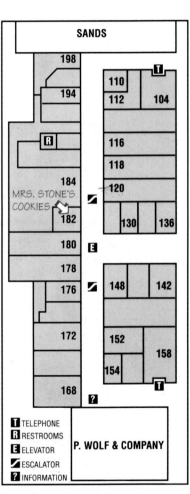

2. Get information. You're at the mall information booth. Ask for the locations of six places you want to go to that aren't numbered on your directory. Then write the names of the stores on your map.

3. Find out about places to shop and eat in your partner's country.

Progress Checks ✔

1. d ☐ Use a mall directory to give directions.

A, cover the numbers on the directory and ask for directions to a place. B, give directions. Don't say the number. A, circle the place on the map.

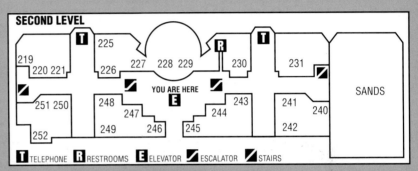

2. a ☐ Change the topic of a conversation.

What are the people saying?

Do it yourself.

3. c ☐ Order a meal from a menu in a restaurant.

A, order a meal. Order at least one item from each column. B, take the order.

BURGERS & HOT SANDWICHES		SIDE DISHES		BEVERAGES			
Hamburger	1.09	Cole Slaw	.59	Cola, Lemon/Lime	.85	.95	1.05
Cheeseburger	1.19	Potato Salad	.69	Orange Juice	.85	.95	1.05
Bacon Cheeseburger	1.59	French Fries	.99	Iced Tea	.85	.95	1.05
Fish Fillet Sandwich	1.89	Onion Rings	1.19	Coffee, Decaf, Tea	.59	.69	.79
Chicken Sandwich	2.79	Garden Salad	1.29	2% Low Fat Milk	.59	.69	.79

Progress Checks

4. b ☐   Read food labels and follow directions for preparing food.

Read the food label. Number the steps in order.

Chicken Noodle Soup

Empty the contents of one envelope of soup mix into a medium saucepan.

■

Slowly stir in 4 cups of water.

■

Bring to a boil, stirring occasionally. Reduce heat and simmer 5 minutes, stirring occasionally.

Problem Solving

What's Tony's problem?

What should Tony do?
Now role play.
What kinds of problems have you had in restaurants?

Getting Started _____

1. Guess. Where is Anda? What is she doing? Who is she calling? What are they saying? What's going to happen next?

 2. What can you hear?

Conversations _____

1. Practice.

Agent: Hello. J & R Realty.
Anda: Hello. I'm looking for a two-bedroom apartment, and I saw some ads in your window. Is anything still available?
Agent: Um. Let me check. Yes. We have a nice two-bedroom in Bridgeton Heights.
Anda: Oh? What's it like?
Agent: Well, it's on the first floor, and it has a large, modern kitchen.
Anda: And how much is the rent?
Agent: $560, plus utilities and a one month security deposit.
Anda: I'm sorry. Did you say utilities are included?
Agent: No. Utilities *aren't* included. And no pets allowed.

2. Talk about apartments. A, call about a one-, two-, or three-bedroom apartment. Use the questions in 1. B, you're a real estate agent. Use the ads.

For Rent-Bridgeton Heights
2 Bedroom Apartment
Large, modern kitchen
#560/month + utilities
1 month's security deposit

For Rent
3 Bedroom, 2 Bath Apt.
Ferndale
Rent #1600, utilities included
1 month's security deposit

J & R REALTY
792 5200
CLOSED

Sunny 1 Bedroom for Rent
Hillside location
Near transportation
#732 includes heat
2 months' security deposit

For Rent
2 Bedroom, 2 Bathroom Apartment
New building-Bridgeton Heights
1250/month + utilities
2 months' security deposit

Large 1 BR Apartment For Rent
in Old House-Hillside
Beautiful garden
#483 + utilities
2 months' security deposit

For Rent-Furnished 3 Bedroom
Mountainview
Across from high school
#1234 + utilities
1 1/2 month's security deposit

For Rent-Ferndale-For Rent
Modern 1 Bedroom/Carpeting
Dishwasher, washer + dryer
#890 + utilities
1 month's security

Downtown 2 Bedroom For Rent
Large rooms
Immediate occupancy
#980 utilities included
1 month's security deposit

WE HAVE MORE APARTMENTS STOP INSIDE FOR DETAILS

Conversations _____

3. Practice.

Manager:	And this is the living room.
Anda:	Well, it's bigger than the living room we have now.
John:	No, it's not, Mom. It's not as big as our living room.
Anda:	It only looks small, John, because there's no furniture in it.
John:	Well, I *still* think our living room is bigger.

4. Focus on grammar.

It's	not	as big as our living room.
	just	

5. Talk about the kitchen, bedroom, apartment, and building. Use these words:

big   bright   modern   quiet   well-kept   cheap

A: What do you think of ___the first kitchen___?

B: Well, it's not as ___modern___ as ___the second kitchen___, but it's

just as ___bright___.

$320 $320

Conversations

6. Practice.

Sonia: I heard about your new apartment! When are you moving?
Anda: I'm not sure. It might not be available until the 15th.
Sonia: Are you going to paint?
Anda: I might, but I haven't made up my mind yet.
Sonia: Well, let me know if you need any help.
Anda: Thanks, Sonia. I can always count on you.

7. Add two words or phrases with similar meanings.

I haven't made up my mind yet.   count on

  I haven't decided yet.   _____

_____   _____

8. Focus on grammar.

Is she going to move on March 1? She	might	move on March 15.
	might not	

9. Talk about Anda's plans for the living room.

A: Is she going to ___paint the living room blue___?

B: She's not sure. She might ___paint it blue___ or she might ___paint it white___.

A: Is she going to ___get a sofa___?

B: Yes, she is.

Paperwork _____

1. **Read the recycling instructions. Circle a word you want to learn. Work with your classmates. Find out what it means.**

How to Prepare Materials for Recycling

Aluminum and Steel Cans

Food and beverage cans only. Rinse thoroughly. You don't need to remove labels or to crush or flatten the cans. Put the cans in plastic bags, tie the bags, and put them in the recycling bin. No paint cans, oil cans, or aerosol cans.

Glass

Food and beverage bottles and jars only. Rinse thoroughly. You can leave labels and metal caps and rings on. Put bottles and jars directly into the recycling bin. No broken glass, light bulbs, or dishes.

Newspapers

All newspapers and newspaper supplements are OK. Tie with string or place in a brown paper bag on top of or beside your recycling bin. No phone books, magazines, or mail.

Plastics

All beverage containers are OK. Rinse thoroughly. Remove caps and flatten containers before you put them in the recycling bin. No shampoo bottles, detergent bottles, or bleach bottles.

Recycling — It's the Law   ♻   Printed on recycled paper

b 2. **Put an X on the items that are *not* OK to recycle. Circle the items that are OK to recycle and ready for recycling. Underline the items that are OK to recycle, but not ready for recycling.**

3. **Add questions with your classmates. Then interview three classmates.**

Do you recycle? What do you recycle? ___Yes. I recycle cans.___

What are the recycling laws in your area? ___We have to recycle cans, glass,___
___newspapers, and plastics.___

_____

4. **Pool your information. Then write summary sentences.**

Reading and Writing _____

1. **Work in pairs. Close your books. What information can you find in a lease? Write your answers.**

2. **Read Anda's lease. Circle a word you want to learn. Work with your classmates. Find out what it means.**

LEASE AGREEMENT – UNFURNISHED APARTMENT

Landlord __Roger Gordon__

Address __2910 Elmont Boulevard, Bridgeton, CA 93204__

Premises __83 Orange Street, Apt. 204, Bridgeton, CA 93202__

Tenant __Anda Boros__

---

1. The LANDLORD leases to the TENANT, __Anda Boros__, the premises described above for a term of __2 years__ beginning __March 1, 1993__ and ending __February 28, 1995__ at a monthly rate of __$560__, payable on the __1st__ day of each month.

2. The tenant shall use the leased premises exclusively as a private residence for no more than __4__ persons, and the tenant shall not make any alterations without the written consent of the landlord.

3. The __tenant__ shall pay for gas and electricity.

4. The tenant agrees to give the landlord a security deposit of __$560__, to be deposited in an interest-bearing account. The landlord shall use the security deposit for the cost of repairing damage, if any, to the premises caused by the tenant.

5. The landlord shall return the security deposit or the balance of the deposit, if any, no later than 10 days after the tenant moves out.

6. The landlord and tenant agree that this apartment lease, when filled out and signed, is a binding legal obligation.

_____   _____
Witness   Landlord

_____   _____
Witness   Tenant

dated this __3rd__ day of __February__, 19__93__.

---

3. **Read the lease again. Check your answers in 1 with a partner.**

c 4. **Work with a partner. Write five questions about the filled-in items in the lease. Use *who, when, how much, how long,* and *how many.***

d 5. **Change partners. Answer your new partner's questions in 4.**

Reading and Writing _____

6. Read the change of address order. Circle a word you want to learn. Work with your classmates. Find out what it means.

U.S. Postal Service **CHANGE OF ADDRESS ORDER**	Customer instructions: Complete Items 1 thru 9. Except Item 8, please PRINT all information.	**OFFICIAL USE ONLY**

1. Change of Address for *(Check one)* ☐ Individual ☐ Entire family ☐ Business

Zone/Route ID no.

2. Start Date
    Month   Day   Year

3. If TEMPORARY address, print date to discontinue forwarding
    Month   Day   Year

Date Entered on Form 3982
Month   Day   Year

4. Print Last Name or Name of Business *(if more than one, use separate Change of Address Order Form for each)*

Expiration Date
Month   Day   Year

5. Print First Name of Head of Household *(include Jr., Sr., etc.)*. Leave blank if the Change of Address Order is for a business.

Clerk/Carrier Endorsement

6. Print **OLD** mailing address, number and street

Apt./Suite No.   P.O. Box No.   R.R/HCR No.   Rural Box/HCR Box No.

City   State   ZIP Code

7. Print **NEW** mailing address, number and street

Apt./Suite No.   P.O. Box No.   R.R/HCR No.   Rural Box/HCR Box No.

City   State   ZIP Code

8. Signature

OFFICIAL USE ONLY

9. Date Signed
    Month   Day   Year

OFFICIAL USE ONLY

Verification Endorsement

7. You're moving into Anda's new apartment building. Complete the change of address order.

8. Write in your journal. Compare housing in the United States and in your country.

Listening Plus _____

1. Listen to the contrast. Point.

Unstressed Auxiliary or _Be_
Utilities aren't included.

Stressed Auxiliary or _Be_
Utilities <u>aren't</u> included.

Underline the auxiliary or _be_ only if it is stressed.

1. It <u>is</u> a furnished apartment.
3. They don't make a lot of money.
5. The furnace is broken.

2. They don't <u>allow</u> pets.
4. The apartment <u>is</u> in perfect condition.
6. She <u>didn't</u> sign the lease.

2. Listen. Number the pictures.

Listen again. What do you think the next speaker will say?

3. You're calling the Recycling Center for information. You live downtown. For each category, write an example of something you can recycle and complete the notes.

Glass	Cans _Sode cans_	Plastics	Paper
Spaghetti sauce jars			

Pick-up Day ___ _Monday_ ___ Time: Place bin at curb by ___ _a.m._ ___ on collection day.

Interactions _____

Student A

1. **You're moving into a new apartment. Arrange the furniture in your living room. Draw the furniture where you want it.**

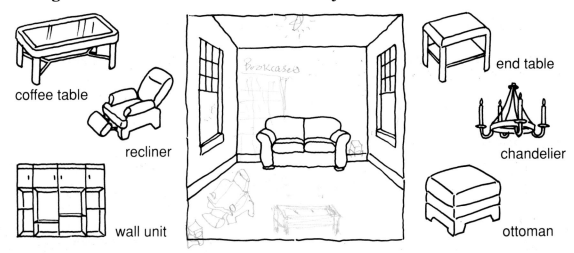

coffee table

recliner

wall unit

end table

chandelier

ottoman

2. **Give information. B is helping you move. Tell B where your furniture goes. Describe the furniture if B doesn't understand.**

A: ___The wall unit goes on the back wall___.

B: ___The wall unit?___ `Li East`

A: ___Yes. The thing that looks like bookcases___.

B: ___Oh, I see. OK. On the back wall. What about the recliner___?

3. **Get information. You're helping B move. Find out where to put B's bedroom furniture. Draw the furniture in the correct place.**

4. **Find out about the last time your partner moved to a new home.**

Interactions

Student B

1. You're moving into a new apartment. Arrange the furniture in your bedroom. Draw the furniture where you want it.

night table

dressing table

dresser

stool

rug

rocking chair

2. Get information. You're helping A move. Find out where to put A's living room furniture. Draw the furniture in the correct place.

    A: ___The wall unit goes on the back wall___ .

    B: ___The wall unit___ ?

    A: ___Yes. The thing that looks like bookcases___ .

    B: ___Oh, I see. OK. On the back wall. What about the recliner___ ?

3. Give information. A is helping you move. Tell A where your furniture goes. Describe the furniture if A doesn't understand.

4. Find out about the last time your partner moved to a new home.

Progress Checks ✔

1. **a** ☐ State your needs and ask specific questions about housing by phone.

What are the people saying?

I'm looking for a _____.

Do it yourself.
Bring in housing ads from the newspaper. A, call B.
B, use the ads.

2. **d** ☐ Read a simplified lease or rental agreement.
   c ☐ Ask questions about a lease or rental agreement.

A, ask five questions about the lease. Use *who, when, how much,*
***how long,* and *how many.* B, answer the questions.**

LEASE AGREEMENT – UNFURNISHED APARTMENT

Landlord Barbara Kremer

Address 2198 12th Avenue, Bridgeton, CA 93205

Premises 412 Elm Street, Apt. B, Bridgeton, CA 93203

Tenant Frances Johnson

1. The LANDLORD leases to the TENANT, ___Frances Johnson___, the premises described above for a term of __1 year__ beginning __July 1, 1994__ and ending __June 30, 1995__ at a monthly rate of __$480__, payable on the __1st__ day of each month.

2. The tenant shall use the leased premises exclusively as a private residence for no more than __2__ persons, and the tenant shall not make any alterations without the written consent of the landlord.

3. The __landlord__ shall pay for gas and electricity.

4. The tenant agrees to give the landlord a security deposit of __$720__, to be deposited in an interest-bearing account. The landlord shall use the security deposit for the cost of repairing damage, if any, to the premises caused by the tenant.

Progress Checks ✔

3. b ☐ Read and follow instructions for recycling.

Read the instructions. Circle the items that are ready for recycling.

HOW TO PREPARE MATERIALS FOR RECYCLING

PLASTICS

Remove caps and rinse thoroughly. Crushing or flattening is not necessary. Large plastic soda bottles only — please do not recycle milk jugs, shampoo or detergent bottles.

CANS

Food and beverage cans only. Please rinse cans thoroughly. You can leave labels on. Flatten or crush the cans. Do not recycle aerosol, paint, or oil cans.

Problem Solving

What's Brenda's problem?

What should Brenda do?
Now role play.
What kinds of problems have you had in apartments?

8 On the Job

Getting Started _____

1. **Guess. Where are Carlos and Sam? What are they doing? What are they saying? What's going to happen next?**

2. **What can you hear?**

Conversations _____

1. Practice.

Sam: What's the problem, Carlos?
Carlos: It's this drawer. It's been jamming all morning. Now it's totally stuck.
Sam: Yeah, I know. It hasn't been working right all week. I guess I have to call the repair guy.
Carlos: That's a good idea. The customers have been complaining.

2. Focus on grammar.

It's	been	jamming	all morning.
It hasn't		working	since 9:00. for the past three hours.

It's = It has

a 3. Talk about the problems. Use any time expressions.

A: What's the problem?
B: It's __these lights__.
   __They've__ been __flickering__ all __afternoon__.
   OR __They've__ been __flickering__ since __lunch time__.
   OR __They've__ been __flickering__ for __the past five hours__.

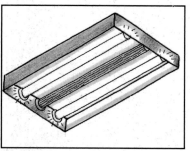

lights/flicker

doors/not work

burglar alarm/ring

speaker/make strange noises

manager/sleep

Conversations _____

4. Practice.

Carlos: What's the matter, Gladys? You look upset.
Gladys: I *am* upset. Sam keeps asking me out.
Carlos: Well, you don't have to go out with him
        if you don't want to.
Gladys: Yeah, but he says I'll lose my job if I don't.
Carlos: He can't fire you for that. It's illegal.
Gladys: It is?
Carlos: Yes. Your boss can't force you to go out
        with him. That's sexual harassment.

5. Add two words or phrases with similar meanings.

upset	*keeps*	*illegal*
disturbed		

6. Talk about employer obligations.

A: Can employers ___force you to retire at age 65___ ?

B: No. They can't ___force you to retire at age 65___ . It's against the law.

    Do employers have to ___provide child care___ ?

A: No. They don't have to ___provide child care___ . But they can if they want to.

Conditional format Conversations

7. Practice.

Gladys:	Sam, can I speak to you for a moment?
Sam:	Sure, Gladys. What can I do for you?
Gladys:	I'm giving you two weeks' notice. My last day is the 25th.
Sam:	What? You're quitting?
Gladys:	That's right.
Sam:	I see. Well, you know, I won't give you a letter of recommendation.
Gladys:	That's OK. I don't need one. I've already accepted another job. Oh, and by the way, I've filed a complaint against you.

8. Talk about quitting. Give notice for quitting a job. Use any date.

A: Can I speak to you for a moment, please?

B: Sure. What can I do for you?

A: I'm giving you two weeks' notice.
   _____I've accepted another job_____.

B: I'm sorry to hear that. When is your last day?

A: _____.

Paperwork _____

1. **Read the safety rules. Circle a word you want to learn. Work with your classmates. Find out what it means.**

_1_ Keep the work area clean.
_2_ Use the right tool.
_3_ Maintain tools with care.
_4_ Store idle tools.
_5_ Guard against electric shock.
_6_ Don't mishandle tools.
_7_ Disconnect tools when not in use.
_8_ Dress properly.
_9_ Use safety goggles.
_10_ Stay alert.

C

2. **Work in pairs. Look at the work area. Circle the safety problems. Write the number of the safety rule that applies.**

3. **Add questions with your classmates. Then interview three classmates.**

   What tools do you know how to operate?   _electric drill, power saw_

   What safety rules must you follow at your job?   _I have to wear safety goggles._

   _____?   _____

4. **Pool your information. Then write summary sentences.**

Reading and Writing _____

1. **Work in pairs. What do you think *benefits* are? Close your books and write your answer.**

2. **Read the benefits summary. Circle a word you want to learn. Work with your classmates. Find out what it means.**

Prince Fabrics, Inc. Summary of Employee Benefits

Paid Vacation
You will receive paid vacation days according to the number of years you have worked here: 1–5 years, 10 days; 6–15 years, 15 days; 16–25 years, 20 days; over 25 years, 25 days. You must use your vacation days by December 31—there can be no carry-over to the next year. All vacation requests must be in writing at least one month before your vacation. First year employees are eligible for paid vacation after four months of employment. For more information, please consult the Personnel Department.

Paid Holidays
You are eligible for paid holidays as soon as you are hired. We now observe nine holidays. You will receive a list of paid holidays each January.

Sick Days
You can take up to eight paid sick days each year for personal or family illness. For illnesses of more than seven consecutive days, see **Disability**.

Disability
Disability leave begins after seven consecutive days of illness. Your physician must fill out a disability form (available from the Personnel Office). Leave for pregnancy or childbirth is the same as any other temporary disability leave.

Worker's Compensation
We carry worker's compensation insurance to protect you in case of injury on the job or as a result of employment. If you are injured on the job, you must file a claim within 20 days of the accident.

---

3. **Read the benefits summary again. Check your answers in 1 with a partner.**

d 4. **Work with a partner. Write *T* for *True*, *F* for *False*, and *?* if the summary of benefits doesn't say.**

a. The day after Thanksgiving is a paid holiday at Prince Fabrics. ____

b. You've been working at Prince Fabrics for three years. You took five vacation days last year. This year you can take 15 days. ____

c. Worker's compensation will pay your full salary if you are injured on the job. ____

d. You can take sick days if your child is sick. ____

Reading and Writing _____

5. **Work with your partner. Look at the memo in 6. What are the differences between a business letter and a memo? Write your answers.**

6. **Read the memo.**

Prince Fabrics, Inc. · 128 Broadway · Bridgeton, California 93204

Memorandum

To: Judith Brent
From: Kevin Dwyer *KD*
Date: January 26, 1995
Subject: Vacation Request

I would like to take vacation from March 15 to 19, 1995.

I hope these dates are convenient. Please let me know as soon as possible.

Thank you.

---

e 7. **Work with your partner. Kevin Dwyer has been working for Prince Fabrics since 1986. Look at the summary of benefits. Did he correctly follow the instructions for requesting a vacation?**

8. **You've been at Prince Fabrics for three years. Write a vacation request memo.**

Prince Fabrics, Inc. · 128 Broadway · Bridgeton, California 93204

Memorandum

To:

From:

Date:

Subject:

---

9. **Write in your journal. Compare employee benefits in the United States and in your country.**

Listening Plus _____

1. Listen to the contrast. Point.

Unstressed Auxiliary or _Be_
People have been complaining.

Stressed Auxiliary or _Be_
People <u>have</u> been complaining.

Underline the auxiliary or _be_ only if it is stressed.

1. You should put it in writing.
2. You can get fired for that.
3. I can't call her.
4. She hasn't been working here long.
5. He was coming.
6. You aren't eligible.

2. Listen. Number the pictures.

Listen again. What do you think the next speaker will say?

3. You're an administrative assistant at Prince Fabrics, Inc. Your boss is out of the office today. He has dictated a memo on your office answering machine. Write the memo.

To:	
From:	
Date:	
Subject:	

Interactions

Student A

1. **Work with other A's. Practice making the paper cup in 2. Don't let the B's see.**

2. **Give information. Give B instructions for making a paper cup. (Don't tell B what it is.) Make sure B is following your instructions. Help B if you need to, but don't show B your pictures.**

   A: __Fold the paper in half__.

   B: __Like this__?

   A: __No. The other way...that's right__.

   B: __OK. Now what__?

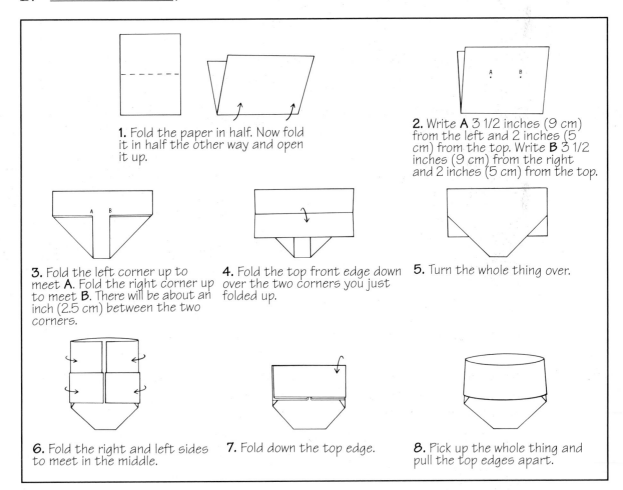

1. Fold the paper in half. Now fold it in half the other way and open it up.

2. Write A 3 1/2 inches (9 cm) from the left and 2 inches (5 cm) from the top. Write B 3 1/2 inches (9 cm) from the right and 2 inches (5 cm) from the top.

3. Fold the left corner up to meet **A**. Fold the right corner up to meet **B**. There will be about an inch (2.5 cm) between the two corners.

4. Fold the top front edge down over the two corners you just folded up.

5. Turn the whole thing over.

6. Fold the right and left sides to meet in the middle.

7. Fold down the top edge.

8. Pick up the whole thing and pull the top edges apart.

3. **Guess. What did you make?**

4. **Get information. Start with a piece of paper the size of this page. Follow B's instructions. Ask for help if you need it.**

Interactions

Student B

1. Work with other B's. Practice making the small envelope in 3. Don't let the A's see.

2. Get information. Start with a piece of paper the size of this page. Follow A's instructions. Ask for help if you need it.

   A: <u>Fold the paper in half</u>.

   B: <u>Like this</u> ?

   A: <u>No. The other way...that's right</u>.

   B: <u>OK. Now what</u> ?

3. Give information. Give A instructions for making a small envelope. (Don't tell A what it is.) Make sure A is following your instructions. Help A if you need to, but don't show A your pictures.

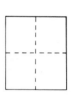

1. Start with a blank piece of paper, the size of this book. Fold the paper in half.

2. Fold all four corners toward the middle.

3. Write A at the two points. Write B where the two corners meet.

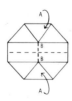

4. Fold both points A to points B.

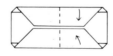

5. Fold the top and bottom to the middle.

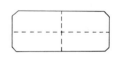

6. Turn the whole thing over.

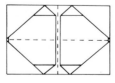

7. Fold the right and the left ends to meet in the middle.

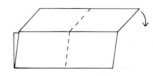

8. Turn the whole thing over again.

9. Fold the top half backward to meet the bottom half.

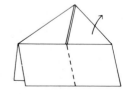

10. You now have two pockets. Look inside. Pull the triangle out of one of the pockets.

4. Guess. What did you make?

Progress Checks ✔

1. **a** ☐ Report and describe problems on the job.

What are the people saying? Do it yourself. Use another problem.

What's the problem?

_____ all morning.

2. **c** ☐ Read safety rules for tools and equipment.

Read the safety rules. Match.

1. Maintain tools with care.
2. Use safety goggles.
3. Store idle tools.
4. Disconnect tools when not in use.
5. Use the right tool.

3. **b** ☐ Give notice for quitting a job.

What are the people saying?

I'm sorry to hear that. When is your last day?

Do it yourself.

Progress Checks ✔

4. **d** ☐ Read personnel policies and employee benefit documents.
  e ☐ Read a simple work memo.

Read the memo. Then answer the questions.

MEMORANDUM

To: All Staff
From: Yuri Ivanov
Date: May 16, 1993
Subject: New Procedure for Worker's Compensation

This is the new procedure for Worker's Compensation. It replaces the information you now have in your handbook.

If you are injured on the job, you must immediately report the accident to your supervisor. For emergency treatment, you must visit a physician, clinic, or health center on the company list. (For a copy of the list, please see the Personnel Director.)

If you are injured on the job and lose more than three days of work, you will be paid disability benefits in accordance with the state's Worker's Compensation laws.

a. If you are injured on the job, when do you have to report the accident?
b. If you are injured on the job, where do you have to go for emergency treatment?
c. When do you get paid disability benefits?

Problem Solving

What's Alberto and Joanne's problem?

What should Alberto and Joanne do?
Now role play.
What kinds of problems have you had at work?

9 Shopping

Getting Started _____

1. **Guess. Where are Sonia and the clerk? What are they doing? What are they saying? What's going to happen next?**

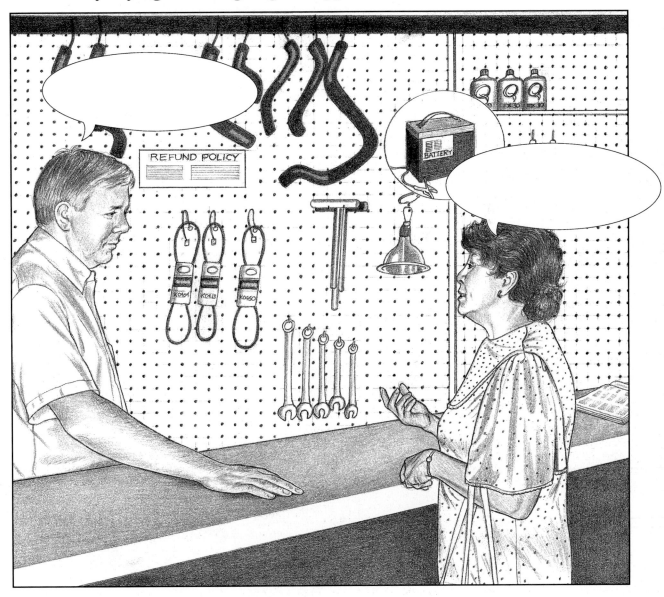

2. **What can you hear?**

Conversations _____

1. Practice.

Clerk: Can I help you?
Sonia: Yes. I need a new battery. How much are they?
Clerk: Well, they range from $40 to $132. It depends on the kind of car you have.
Sonia: Oh. I have a 1988 Dodge Colt.
Clerk: Hold on a minute and I'll look it up for you. Then you can just go to Aisle 3B and pick out the one you want.
Sonia: Thanks a lot.
Clerk: Sure thing.

2. Add two words or phrases with similar meanings.

Hold on a minute.	*pick out*	*Sure thing.*
_____	choose	_____
_____	_____	_____

3. Talk about car parts.

A: Can I help you?

B: Yes. I need a new _battery_.
How much are they?

A: They range from _$40 to $132_.

$40–$132 $5–$18 $8–$12

$5–$25 $6–$7

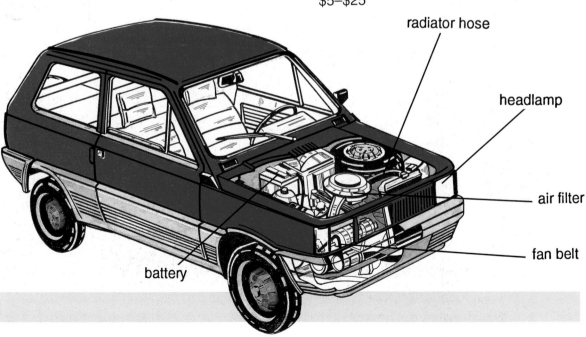

radiator hose

headlamp

air filter

fan belt

battery

Conversations _____

4. Practice.

Officer: What happened, ma'am?
Sonia: Someone broke into the trunk of my car. Well, actually, it's my son's car. I was shopping at Peer's. I was only gone for about 15 minutes.
Officer: Uh-huh. What exactly was taken?
Sonia: Tools. My son kept a toolbox in the trunk.
Officer: Do you know the value of the property?
Sonia: No. I'll have to call you later.
Officer: OK, but I need some information now. Your name?

BRIDGETON POLICE DEPARTMENT TO SERVE AND PROTECT

COMPLAINT REPORT

OFFENSE _car break in_

TIME _10:00 AM_   DATE _5/15/95_

LOCATION _Westside Mall Parking Lot N15_

NAME _López_   _Sonia_   M
Last   First   MI

TYPE OF PROPERTY _Tools_   VALUE _Unknown_

5. Talk about a theft. A, you're a police officer. Ask questions. B, choose one of the situations.

A: What happened?

B: Someone ___broke into my car___.

A: _____.

BRIDGETON POLICE DEPARTMENT TO SERVE AND PROTECT

COMPLAINT REPORT

OFFENSE _____

TIME _____ DATE _____

LOCATION _____

NAME _____
Last   First   MI

TYPE OF PROPERTY _____ VALUE _____

broke into my car

snatched my purse

picked my pocket

stole my shopping bag

took my bike

Conversations

6. Practice.

Meng: I heard about what happened, Sonia. What a shame.
Sonia: Yeah. My son was really upset, but I wasn't. After all, I wasn't hurt. Well, anyway, how was *your* weekend?
Meng: Not bad. I went shopping at Sands. They were having a sale.
Sonia: They have good prices, don't they? I usually shop at Wolf's, though.
Meng: Oh, yeah? Why's that?
Sonia: They have a lot of things in my size, but Sands doesn't.

7. Focus on grammar.

Sands **had**	a sale,	but Wolf's	**didn't.**
Wolf's **didn't have**	a sale,	but Sands	**did.**
Sands **doesn't have**	my size,	but Wolf's	**does.**
Wolf's **has**	my size,	but Sands	**doesn't.**

8. Talk about the stores.

A: Where did you go shopping, _Wolf's or Sands_?

B: _Sands. They were having a sale, but Wolf's wasn't_.

were having a sale

are open Sundays

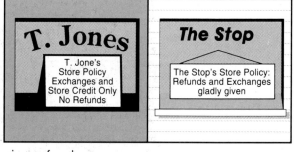

give refunds

accept credit cards

stay open all night

Paperwork

1. **Read the check. Circle a word you want to learn. Work with your classmates. Find out what it means.**

		10275
Sonia López **10298 Lincoln Avenue, Apt. C** **Bridgeton, CA 93204**		_June 11_ 19 _95_

    PAY TO THE ORDER OF _Wolf's_ _____ $ _95.86_

    Ninety five and ⁸⁶/₁₀₀ _____—DOLLARS

    The Bridgeton National Bank
    123 Main Street, Bridgeton, CA 93204

    MEMO _____ _Sonia López_

b

2. **You're shopping at Sands. Your purchases total $185.99. Write a check.**

		1125
Ernilla Lotel 10108 Tibalsn St., Aprt.naith 5 Bridtvond Dr stn 11118		_____ 19 ____

    PAY TO THE ORDER OF _____ $ [   ]

    _____ DOLLARS

    NatBank
    123 Street, Btrn, AM 90004

    MEMO _____

3. **Add questions with your classmates. Then interview three classmates.**

    Do you have a checking account? — Yes, at Broadway Bank

    What do you pay for by check? — rent, utility bills

    How do you pay for your purchases at stores? — cash or credit card

    _____? _____

4. **Pool your information. Then write summary sentences.**

Reading and Writing _____

1. **What is a warranty? What do you own that has a warranty? Discuss with your class.**

2. **Read the warranty. Circle a word you want to learn. Work with your classmates. Find out what it means.**

PLYMOUTH ELECTRONICS
▪ LIMITED WARRANTY ▪
Warranty Valid Only in Country of Product Purchase

What This Warranty Covers

Plymouth USA and Plymouth of Canada will repair or replace all car radios that fail to function properly under normal use due to manufacturing defect, without charge for parts or labor, for a period of one year from the date of purchase.

What's Not Covered

This warranty does not cover the cabinet or any antennas you have attached. It does not cover any damage to the radio resulting from alterations, accident, misuse or abuse, or lightning. This warranty does not cover defects or damage caused by the use of unauthorized parts or labor, or from improper maintenance.

To Obtain Service

Only authorized Plymouth Service Companies can provide service. (See reverse for list.) To receive warranty service, you will need to present your sales receipt. If you have to ship the radio, you will need to package it carefully, pay for shipping, and send it to an Authorized Service Company. Include in the package, your name, address, daytime phone number, a copy of your sales receipt, and a detailed description of the problem.

RECORD THE PLACE AND DATE OF PURCHASE FOR FUTURE REFERENCE

Model No. _____ Serial No. _____ Purchase Date _____

Purchased From _____

---

c 3. **Work with your partner. Which of these situations does the warranty cover? Circle the letters.**

a. The radio is two months old. It's damaged in an accident.
b. The radio is three months old. It stops working.
c. The radio is five months old. It's damaged in a thunderstorm.
d. The radio is seven months old. The cabinet gets scratched when you remove the radio from your car.
e. The radio is ten months old. You can't change stations.

Reading and Writing

4. Work with your partner. Label the pictures with the problems.

broken   bent   torn   cracked

   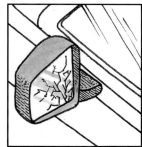

child safety seat   windshield wipers   floor mats   sideview mirror

_____ _____ _____ _____

5. Read the letter. Circle a word you want to learn. Work with your classmates. Find out what it means.

```
                        10298 Lincoln Avenue, Apt. C
                        Bridgeton, CA  93204

                        May 11, 1996

Customer Service Department
AutoMotive, Inc.
P.O. Box  3219
Edison, NJ  08817

Dear Customer Service Department:

        I am returning a pair of your deluxe
windshield wipers, which I bought on May 4,
1996 at R&S Auto Palace, Bridgeton, CA.  I
have enclosed a copy of my sales slip.

        When I took the wipers out of the
package, I noticed they were bent.

        Please send me a replacement pair.
Thank you.

                    Sincerely yours,

                    Sonia López
                    Sonia López

Enclosure
```

d **6. Choose one of the other products in 4 and write a letter to request a replacement.**

Listening Plus _____

1. **Listen to the contrast. Point.**

Question	**Comment** _____
They have good prices, <u>don't</u> they?	They have good prices, don't <u>they?</u>

Write *Q* for *Question* and *C* for *Comment*.

1. That's a good price, isn't it? ⌐ 2. They're open late, aren't they? __

3. You give refunds, don't you? __ 4. It's expensive, isn't it? __

5. It's on Route 4, isn't it? __ 6. That happened to Al too, didn't it? __

2. **Listen. Number the pictures.**

Listen again. What do you think the next speaker will say?

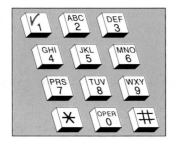

3. Call Sands department store for information about your Sands charge account. Use the keypad. Instead of pushing a button, check (√) it. Your account number is 14-311-23-616.

Available credit: _____

Account balance: _____

Date of last payment Sands received: _____

Interactions _____

Student A

1. **Give information. Answer the phones at these auto service centers. Answer B's questions.**

   A: ___P & F Service___.

   B: Hello. I have a ___1991 Ford Escort___, and I need ___a tune-up, an oil change, and a cooling system flush___.

   A: I'm sorry. You need ___a tune-up___ and what else?

   B: _____.

P & F Service Price List	
Brake Job	$200.00
Oil Change	$22.00
Front-End Alignment	$39.00
Tune-up	$100.00
Rear Shock Absorbers	$60.00
Cooling System Flush	$40.00

Links Auto Service Price List	
Brake Job	$187.00
Oil Change	$ 26.25
Front-End Alignment	$ 49.00
Tune-up	$ 44.00
Rear Shock Absorbers	$ 85.00
Cooling System Flush	$ 59.95

Bertoli Brothers Price List	
Brake Job	$194.00
Oil Change	$16.25
Front-End Alignment	$39.00
Tune-up	$39.99
Rear Shock Absorbers	$79.00
Cooling System Flush	$39.50

Appointment: Tomorrow
Time needed for work: 4hrs

Appointment: Before 1:00 p.m. Time needed for work: 2hrs

Appointment: Right away
Time needed for work: 3 hrs

e 2. **Get information. You have a 1992 Toyota Celica. It needs a brake job, front-end alignment, and new rear shock absorbers. Call these auto service centers and comparison-shop.**

Name of Service Center:	Bob's Auto Repair	Auto World	Westside Auto Service
Costs:			
Brake job			
Front-end alignment			
Rear shock absorbers			
When can I bring it in?			
How long will it take?			

3. **Which place are you going to take your car to? Tell your partner why.**

Interactions

Student B

e 1. **Get information. You have a 1991 Ford Escort. It needs a tune-up, an oil change, and a cooling system flush. Call these auto service centers and comparison-shop.**

A: <u>P & F Service</u>.

B: Hello. I have a <u>1991 Ford Escort</u>, and I need <u>a tune-up, an oil change,</u> <u>and a cooling system flush</u>.

A: I'm sorry. You need <u>a tune-up</u> and what else?

B: _____.

Name of Service Center:	*P & F Service*	*Links Auto Service*	*Bertoli Brothers*
Costs:			
Tune-up			
Oil Change			
Cooling system flush			
When can I bring it in?			
How long will it take?			

2. **Give information. Answer the phones at these auto service centers. Answer A's questions.**

Bob's Auto Repair Price List

Brake Job	$189.00
Oil Change	$18.00
Front-end Alignment	$44.00
Tune-up	$100.00
Rear Shock Absorbers	$60.00
Cooling System Flush	$40.00

Appointment: Tomorrow a.m. Time needed for work: 5 hrs

Auto World Price List

Brake Job	$187.00
Oil Change	$22.00
Front-end Alignment	$39.00
Tune-up	$50.00
Rear Shock Absorbers	$69.00
Cooling System Flush	$49.00

Appointment: Before 12:00 p.m. Time needed for work: 3 hrs

Westside Auto Service Price List

Brake Job	$194.00
Oil Change	$26.25
Front-end Alignment	$49.00
Tune-up	$44.00
Rear Shock Absorbers	$79.00
Cooling System Flush	$39.00

Appointment: Right away Time needed for work: 6 hrs

3. **Which place are you going to take your car to? Tell your partner why.**

Progress Checks ✔

1. **b** ☐ Write a check.

You're ordering sheepskin car seat covers from AutoMotive, Inc. Write a check for $73.95.

	1125
Smilla Lotel	
10008 Tibalsn St., Aprt.nalth. 5	_____ 19 _____
Findvond Drstr. 11 03	
PAY TO THE	
ORDER OF _____	$ [ ]
	DOLLARS
_____	
NatBank	
123 Street, Bitsl, AM, 90004	
MEMO _____	_____

2. **c** ☐ Read a product warranty.

Read AutoMotive, Inc.'s warranty on the sheepskin car seat covers you ordered.

> **Limited Warranty**
>
> AutoMotive, Inc. will repair or replace your sheepskin car seat covers free of charge for three months from the date of purchase if they fail due to defective workmanship or materials. Please complete and return the warranty registration card to AutoMotive, Inc.
>
> This warranty gives you specific legal rights, and you may also have other rights which vary from state to state.
>
> For service: Please send the defective sheepskin car seat covers to Customer Service Department, AutoMotive, Inc., P. O. Box 3219, Edison, NJ 08817.

True or False? AutoMotive, Inc. will repair or replace your sheepskin car seat covers if:

_____ you spilled coffee on the seat covers and you can't get the stain out.
_____ they were dirty when you took them out of the package.
_____ you've had the seat covers for four months and the straps have broken.

3. **d** ☐ Write a letter to request a replacement.

Your sheepskin car seat covers were dirty when you took them out of the package. Write to AutoMotive, Inc. to request a replacement for them.

Progress Checks ✔

4. **a** ☐ Report a theft.

A, you're a police officer. Ask questions and take notes. B, report a theft.

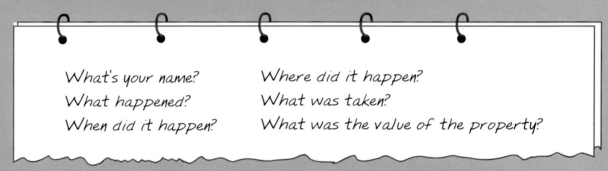

What's your name?　　　Where did it happen?

What happened?　　　　What was taken?

When did it happen?　　What was the value of the property?

5. **e** ☐ Use the phone to find out about products and services.

Call an auto service center. Find out their hours and the cost of a tune-up on your own car or an '91 Buick Skylark.

Problem Solving

What's the problem?

What should Erica do?
Now role play.
What kinds of problems have you had shopping?

10 Community Services

Getting Started _____

1. Guess. Where are Debra and the class? What are they doing? What are they saying? What's going to happen next?

2. What can you hear?

Conversations

1. Practice.

Debra: As I told you last week, on Wednesday night we're going to have class at the library. Do any of you have a library card?
Manny: I do.
Meng: So do I.
Carlos: I do, too.
Debra: Great! And the rest of you can apply for one then.

2. Focus on grammar.

Manny **has been** to the library.	Manny **raised** his hand.
So has Meng.	**So did** Meng.
Carlos **has, too.**	Carlos **did, too.**

3. Work in groups. Talk about the people in the class.

A: <u>Have</u> any of the students <u>ever been to their local library</u>?
B: <u>Manny has</u>.
C: <u>So has Carlos</u>.
D: <u>And Sonia has, too</u>.

A: <u>Do</u> any of the students <u>have a library card</u>?
B: <u>Manny does</u>.
C: <u>So does Meng</u>.
D: <u>And Carlos does, too</u>.

COMMUNITY SERVICES CLASS SURVEY

	Manny	Anda	Chen	Meng	Sonia	Lucy	Carlos	Marco
Have you ever been to your local library?	✓		✓	✓	✓	✓	✓	✓
Do you have a library card?	✓			✓			✓	
Have you ever borrowed books from the library?	✓			✓			✓	
Are you registered to vote in the U.S.?	✓	✓	✓			✓		✓
Did you vote in the last election?	✓	✓	✓			✓		
Will you vote in the next election?	✓	✓	✓			✓		✓
Do you have a driver's license?	✓		✓	✓	✓		✓	✓
Do you belong to the Parent-Teachers Organization?	✓	✓	✓	✓				

Conversations

4. Practice.

Librarian: So those are some of the programs and services we offer. Now are there any questions?

Marco: How long can you borrow a video for?

Librarian: Just overnight.

Carlos: Hey, Marco. You'd better find out about the fee for overdue videos.

Marco: Thanks a lot, Carlos!

5. Add two words or phrases with similar meanings.

offer	*you'd better*	*fee*
	you ought to	

6. Talk about the public library. Find out about library services.

A: Can you borrow videotapes ?

B: Yes.

A: How much does it cost if your book is overdue ?

BRIDGETON PUBLIC LIBRARY
FERNDALE BRANCH

Hours: Monday–Friday 10–7, Saturday and Sunday 11–5

You can borrow
- books
- records, cassettes, and CDs
- videotapes

You cannot borrow
- reference books
- newspapers
- magazines

Large print and foreign language books are available.

You can
- borrow a book for 3 weeks.
- renew a book for an additional 2 weeks.
- return a book to any branch.

Late fee for overdue books: 10¢ per day

We can
- reserve a book for you.
- order a book from another branch.

Conversations _____

7. Practice.

Librarian: And you know, there are five branches in addition to this one.
Meng: They all have the same hours, don't they?
Librarian: No, as a matter of fact, they don't. For example, we're open on Sunday, but the Bridgeton Heights branch isn't. Neither is the Westside branch.
Carlos: I'm not surprised. The branch near me isn't either.
Librarian: Yeah, it really varies. Before you leave, I'll give you a pamphlet. It summarizes the different branch services.

8. Focus on grammar.

This branch **isn't** open on Sundays. **Neither is** the Westside branch. The Mountainview branch **isn't, either.**	This branch **won't be** open on Election Day. **Neither will** the Westside branch. The Mountainview branch **won't, either.**

9. Talk about the library branches.

A: _____ The Hillside branch is n't _____ open on Sundays _____.

B: I'm not surprised.
_____ The Westside branch is n't either. OR Neither is the Westside branch.

C: But _____ the Ferndale branch is _____.

	Ferndale	Hillside	Westside	Downtown
Open Sundays?	✔	✘	✘	✔
Open Election Day?	✘	✔	✘	✘
German Language Books?	✘	✘	✘	✔
Special Activities for Children?	✔	✘	✔	✘
Large Print Books?	✘	✘	✘	✔
Wheelchair Accessible?	✘	✘	✔	✘

Unit 10

Paperwork _____

1. **Read the government page from the Bridgeton phone book. Circle a word you want to learn. Work with your classmates. Find out what it means.**

BRIDGETON, CITY OF (Cont'd.)		Programs		Speech & Hearing Impaired	302-8166
LIBRARY		Arts and Cultural Programs	489-3782	Crime Prevention	489-6488
Downtown Library 22 Jefferson		Day Camp Programs	489-4069	Detective Bureau	489-2127
Recorded Information	489-2000	Senior Citizens Nutritional Progs	489-3778	Narcotics Bureau	489-2165
Children's Library	489-2035	Senior Citizen Hotline	489-3771	Traffic Accident Information	489-2009
Films	489-2033	Sports and Athletics Program	489-3797	Youth Bureau	489-4844
Literacy Office	489-6450	Volunteer Programs	489-2002	PRIVATE INDUSTRY COUNCIL	489-6000
Information Services	489-2043	Facilities Reservations		PUBLIC SERVICE 119 Lincoln	
Library Branches		Building & Facility Reservations	489-2147	Bridgeton Gas and Electric	489-3219
Bridgeton Heights	489-2051	Picnic Reservations	489-2147	Gas Emergencies	489-7400
Ferndale	489-2052	Wedding Site Reservations	489-2147	SANITATION BUREAU	
Hillside	489-2053	Parks and Facilities		Recycling Program	489-7927
Mountainview	489-2054	Administrative Offices 613 Union	489-2110	Refuse Collection	489-8523
Westside	489-2055	Park Maintenance Office 541 Elm	489-2054	Sewer Maintenance	489-8526
MAYOR'S OFFICE	489-4844	Adult Recreation Center 20 12 Av	489-3775	SCHOOLS-PUBLIC	
NEIGHBORHOOD SERVICES	489-3700	Bridgeton Arts Center 683 Park	489-3782	To call a school, look under	
PARAMEDICS	489-4800	Bridgeton Hts. Park Tennis Courts		name of school	
	OR 911	9287 Jefferson	489-4550	TRAFFIC SIGNAL FAILURE	
PARKS RECREATION &		Senior Citizens Center 593 4 Ave	489-8231	After 5 pm	489-3261
COMMUNITY SERVICES		POLICE DEPARTMENT 923 Union	489-2101	TRANSPORTATION PROGRAMS	
General Information 613 Union	489-3000	Emergency	911	Dial-A-Ride Information	489-0329

b 2. **Work in pairs. What number do you call if you want information about:**

a. the Westside branch of the library? _____

b. day camp programs? _____

c. the recycling program? _____

d. picnic reservations? _____

e. crime prevention? _____

3. **Add questions with your classmates. Then interview three classmates.**

Have you ever used the government pages in your phone book? ___*yes*___

If so, what numbers have you looked up? ___*a health care center*___

What kinds of local, state, or federal community services have you used? ___*health care center, parks, library, police, post office*___

4. **Pool your information. Then write summary sentences.**

Reading and Writing _____

1. Look at the calendar of events from the Bridgeton Heights Community Newsletter. On what date can you attend an event on these topics?

health _____   music _____

world news _____   crime prevention _____

sports _____   money _____

2. Read the calendar of events. Circle a word you want to learn. Work with your classmates. Find out what it means.

3. Check your answers in 1 with a partner.

C 4. A, write five questions about the events in 2. For example, *Where does the current events discussion take place?* B, answer A's questions.

Reading and Writing _____

5. **Read the newsletter from Debra's class. Circle a word you want to learn. Work with your classmates. Find out what it means.**

WESTSIDE COMMUNITY ADULT SCHOOL LEVEL 4 CLASS NEWSLETTER

A Message from Debra

It's now the end of the school year, and time for a break from classes. Our past few months together have been fun and a great learning experience for me. I wish you all the best of luck. Stay in touch.

Debra

——— *Where Do We Go From Here?* ———

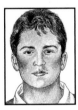 **Carlos** is hoping to change jobs this summer. He's planning to get his GED in the fall.

 **Marco** is going to continue working as a cook at Brasilia. He's inviting us all to his house for a July 4th barbecue.

 **Sonia** is going to Mexico for a few weeks to see her niece's new baby and spend time with her family.

 **Chen** just got a new job, so he can't take a vacation. But he's going to take his family on weekend trips to the mountains.

 **Manny's** son is graduating from high school. The whole family is going to take a trip to Colorado this summer.

 **Meng** isn't going to do anything special this summer. She is going to take her children to the park and swimming pool.

 **Anda** is going to open her own hair and nail salon in the fall. She's going to spend her summer getting ready.

 **Lucy** is taking her daughter to Los Angeles for a week to see her sister. She's going to enter a job training program in the fall.

6. **Interview your classmates and write a class newsletter.**

Listening Plus _____

 1. Listen to the contrast. Point.

Question	**Comment**
It isn't open, is it?	It isn't open, is it?

Write *Q* for *Question* or *C* for *Comment*.

1. They're fast, too, aren't they? __
2. It's free, isn't it? __
3. You don't need one, do you? __
4. It's 911 everywhere, isn't it? __
5. You can use one there, can't you? __
6. It was great, wasn't it? __

 2. Listen. Number the pictures.

Listen again. What do you think the next speaker will say?

d **3. Call the Bridgeton Public Library. Get information and take notes.**

Location: _____

Hours: _____

For information about overdue books or fines, call _____

For reference questions, call _____

For the Children's Library, call _____

Interactions

Student A

1. **Look at the map. Before you get or give information, complete the chart for Newton. Write _Y_ for _Yes_ and _N_ for _No_.**

	Newton	Sunrise
golf courses	N	N
parks	Y	Y
a clinic	Y	N
a zoo		
an aquarium		
beaches		
a swimming pool		
libraries		
tennis courts		
botanical gardens		
playgrounds		
a community college		

(Map showing: Water Street, Long Lake, Snake River, Miles 0–2 scale, compass N/W/E/S, Elm Street, Forest Avenue, Oak Street, Route 22, Church Street, Pine Street.)

2. **Give information about Newton. Complete the chart for Sunrise.**

   A: Newton doesn't have any golf courses.
   B: Neither does Sunrise. OR Sunrise doesn't either.
       Sunrise has a lot of parks.
   A: So does Newton. OR Newton does, too.
       Newton has a clinic. But Sunrise doesn't.

   B: _____.

3. **Decide together. You can move to Newton or Sunrise. Based on the chart, which would you prefer? What other information do you need in order to decide?**

Interactions

Student B

1. **Look at the map. Before you get or give information, complete the chart for Sunrise. Write *Y* for *Yes* and *N* for *No*.**

		Newton	Sunrise
	golf courses	N	N
	parks	Y	Y
	a clinic	Y	N
	a zoo		
	an aquarium		
	beaches		
	a swimming pool		
	libraries		
	tennis courts		
	botanical gardens		
	playgrounds		
	a community college		

Map labels: Water Street, Main Street, Second Street, Third Street, Inland Avenue, Ocean Avenue, River Blvd., Pine Street, 12, The Ocean, 0 Miles 2, N W E S

2. **Give information about Sunrise. Complete the chart for Newton.**

   A: Newton doesn't have any golf courses.
   B: Neither does Sunrise.   OR   Sunrise doesn't either.
      Sunrise has a lot of parks.
   A: So does Newton.   OR   Newton does, too.
   B: _____.

3. **Decide together. You can move to Newton or Sunrise. Based on the chart, which would you prefer? What other information do you need in order to decide?**

Progress Checks ✔

1. **a** ☐ Find out about services provided by a public library.

    Find out the following about your public library:

    a. How long can you borrow a book for? _____

    b. Can you borrow videos or records? _____

    c. What's the late fee for overdue books? _____

    d. What are the hours of the branch nearest your home?

       _____

    e. Add a question of your own: _____?

       _____

2. **b** ☐ Use the government pages of the phone book to find information
    sources for community services.

    Read the government pages from your local phone book.

    **Write the telephone number you would call if you want
    information about:**

    a. adult education programs   _____

    b. job training programs   _____

    c. sports programs   _____

    d. recycling   _____

    e. crime prevention programs   _____

    c. fire safety programs   _____

3. **d** ☐ Get information about community services over the phone.

    **You want information about one of the services in 2. Prepare
    questions. Then call and take notes.**

Progress Checks

4. c ☐ Read information about community services in a community newsletter.

Read the Bridgeton Heights Community Newsletter for the week of May 16.

Monday, May 17
Parent–Teachers Organization Bake Sale
The Parent–Teachers Organization of the Martin Luther King, Jr. School will hold a bake sale in the basement of the school from 3:00 p.m. to 5:00 p.m.

Tuesday, May 18
Fire Safety for Senior Citizens
Inspector William L. Boyle of the Bridgeton Fire Department will explain what to do if fire strikes. A free information book will be distributed. Senior Citizens Center 1:00–2:00 p.m.

Thursday, May 20
Book Club
The Bridgeton Heights Library will hold its monthly book club meeting. Open to all high school students. 4:00–5:00 p.m. Community Room.

Friday, May 21
Free Hearing Tests
Screenings for children three years old and older will be conducted at the Bridgeton Heights Clinic. Tests last about five minutes. No appointments necessary.

Write the dates of the events that are appropriate for:

a. children _____

b. adults _____

c. teenagers _____

d. adults over 60 _____

Problem Solving

What's George's problem?

What should George do?
Now role play.

Grammar Summaries

Irregular Past Tense (review)

My sister	drove	a bus.		She	didn't	drive	a truck.
I	went	to Japan.		I		go	to Korea.

Did	she	drive	a school bus?		When		did	she	drive a bus?
	you	go	to Taiwan?		What countries			you	go to?

Past Continuous Tense with *when* (review)

Pat and Sue	were wearing their seat belts	when	the yellow car hit them.
The blue car	was doing at least 40		the accident happened.

Comparisons of Adverbs

slowly	more	slowly	than	fast	faster	than
carefully		carefully		well	better	
dangerously		dangerously		badly	worse	

Future Time with *be* + verb + *ing* (review)

Are you	doing anything Saturday night?	I'm	taking my mother to the airport.
Is John	getting tickets to the soccer game?	No, we're	going to the movies on Sunday.

Future Time with *will* (review)

I'll be	at my sister's house tomorrow morning.
I won't be	

When will you be home?

Will she be home around 12:00?

Present Perfect Tense

Have	you	given her any medication?	Yes, I have.
			No, I haven't.
Has	her fever	gone down?	Yes, it has.
			No, it hasn't.

Equatives

It's	not	as big as our living room.
	just	

Might

Is she going to move on March 1?	She	might	move on March 15.
		might not	

Present Perfect Continuous Tense

It's	been	jamming	all morning.
It hasn't		working	since 9:00. the past three hours.

It's = It has

Sentence Additions with *but*

Sands **had**	a sale, but Wolf's	**didn't.**
Wolf's **didn't**	have a sale, but Sands	**did.**
Sands **doesn't**	have my size, but Wolf's	**does.**
Wolf's **has**	my size, but Sands	**doesn't.**

Sentence Additions with too, not /either, so, neither

Manny **has been** to the library.
So has Meng.
Carlos **has, too.**

Manny **raised** his hand.
So did Meng.
Carlos **did, too.**

This branch **isn't** open on Sundays.
Neither **is** the West side branch.
The Mountainview branch **isn't** either.

This branch **won't be** open on Election Day.
Neither **will** the Westside branch.
The Mountainview branch **won't,** either.

Present Perfect Tense with *ever*

Have you ever had German measles?	Yes. I had German measels	in 1992. last year.
	No. I've never had German measels.	

I've = I have

she's = she has

he's = he has

you've = you have

we've = we have

they've = they have

Regular and Irregular Past Participles

He's	**had**	a lot of experience.
	installed	heaters.
	repaired	sinks.

answer	answered	**answered**	do	did	**done**
help	helped	**helped**	make	made	**made**
type	typed	**typed**	sell	sold	**sold**
use	used	**used**	take	took	**taken**

Present Perfect Tense with *for* and *since*

How long have you been a salesperson?	For	four years. six months.
	Since	1990. March.

Present Perfect Tense with *already* and *yet* vs. Simple Past Tense with *just*

Have they eaten yet?	She's **already** eaten.	She ate at 6:00.
	He hasn't eaten **yet.**	He **just** ordered.

Indirect *Wh*-questions with *Be*

Where is the phone?	Can you tell me	where the phone is?
What are your specials?		what your specials are?

Tapescript

UNIT 1   Page 8   Listening Plus.

Exercise 1. Listen to the contrast.

He was in her class.
He was in her class?

Exercise 1. Point.

Point to *statement* or *question*.

He's from Brazil.
He's from Brazil?
He's from Brazil?
They got divorced?
They got divorced.
They got divorced?
Her name is Meng?
Her name is Meng.
Her name is Meng.
That's her daughter?
That's her daughter?
That's her daughter.
She drove a bus.
She drove a bus?
She drove a bus.
You came here alone?
You came here alone.
You came here alone?

Exercise 1. Write a period or a question mark at the end of each sentence.

Look at each sentence in your book. When you hear it in the conversation, add a period or question mark.

1.
   A: Why don't you ask Amy?
   B: Amy?
   A: Sure. Amy knows him. She was in his class.

2.
   A: Who's that woman over there?
   B: Oh. That's Cathy Dorsey.
   A: That's our teacher? (as confirmation, not surprise)
   B: Mm-mm.

3.
   A: Didn't Shu Hung sell electronic equipment in Taiwan?
   B: No. He sold cars.

4.
   A: Does Tony know Sandra?
   B: Uh-huh. They met in 1991.

5.
   A: I think Olga and Miguel met when they were students in Guadalajara.
   B: They're from Mexico? I thought they were from Honduras.

6.
   A: Do you know anything about her mother?
   B: She was a physician in China.
   A: Oh. She was a doctor?
   B: Yes. She worked in a children's hospital.

Exercise 2. Listen. Number the pictures.

Write the number of the conversation that matches each picture.

Conversation 1.

A: Hi, there. Great party, huh?
B: Sure is. So, how do you know Al?
A: Oh, we've worked together for years. What about you?

B: Al's my cousin.
A: You're Al's cousin?
B: Yeah. My name's Pete.
A: Hi, Pete. I'm Lucy.
B: Nice to meet you.

Conversation 2.

A: Hello, I'm Cynthia Rotell.
B: Tom Baretta. Nice to meet you.
A: Why don't you have a seat, Mr... Baretto?
B: Baretta.
A: Sorry. Would you like a cup of coffee?
B: That would be great.
A: Milk? Sugar?

Conversation 3.

A: Hello. My name is John Marshall.
B: I'm Laura Newman. How do you do, John?
A: Pleased to meet you, Mrs. Newman. I've heard a lot about you.
B: I've heard a lot about *you*. You did all the cooking for the party?
A: That's right.
B: Everything tastes wonderful.

Conversation 4.

A: Hi. My name is David Robertson. You're a new student, aren't you?
B: Yes. I'm Joyce Duval.
A: Nice to meet you, Joyce.
B: Nice to meet you, Professor Robertson.
A: Oh, please call me by my first name. We're pretty informal around here.
B: Oh, OK. Is that Dave or David?

Exercise 2. Listen again. What do you think the next speaker will say?

Listen to the conversations again. Predict what the next speaker will say.

Exercise 3. You are the secretary at the Westside Community Adult School. Play the messages on the school's answering machine. Fill in the information.

(Answering machine) Thank you for calling the Westside Community Adult School. Our offices are open between the hours of 7:30 a.m. and 7:00 p.m., Monday through Friday. If you want to leave a message, please leave your name, number and the day and time of your call. Remember to speak slowly and wait for the tone.

Hello. This is Pedro Gonzalez. I'm calling to get some information about classes for my niece. I can't be reached during the day, but you can get me at home most evenings. My number there is 798-4328. Oh, it's Monday evening, 7:45. The name, again, is Pedro Gonzalez, P-E-D-R-O G-O-N-Z-A-L-E-Z. Thank you.

Hi. My name is Linda Chen. That's Linda, L-I-N-D-A, Chen, C-H-E-N. I'm a student in Ken Fisher's class. Please tell Ken that I can't come to class tomorrow. I have to take my daughter to the doctor. My number is 837-4930, but Ken doesn't have to call me back. It's now Monday night, around 9:00 p.m. Thanks.

This is Stan De Vito, the plumber, returning your call at 7:00, Tuesday morning. I just got your message from my service. I can be at your school in the afternoon. My number is 450-3847 and the name is Stan, S-T-A-N De Vito, capital D-E, capital V-I-T-O. OK. Talk to you later.

UNIT 2   Page 20   Listening Plus.

Exercise 1. Listen to the contrast.

He drove right through that stop sign.
He drove right through that stop sign?

Exercise 1. Point.

Point to *statement* or *question*.

She was speeding?
She was speeding?
She was speeding.
It's a used car.
It's a used car?
It's a used car?
He had an accident?
He had an accident.
He had an accident?
She got her license.
She got her license?
She got her license?
He was doing 40.
He was doing 40?
He was doing 40.
They were wearing their seatbelts?
They were wearing their seatbelts?
They were wearing their seatbelts.

Exercise 1. Write a period or a question mark at the end of each sentence.

Look at each sentence in your book. When you hear it in the conversation, add a period or question mark.

1.
   A: Have you seen Marta's new car?
   B: Marta got a new car?
   A: Yeah. It's a Honda Accord.
   B: Oh. That's the same car I have. What color is it?

2.
   A: I heard that Bill got a speeding ticket.
   B: Really? Bill's a good driver.
   A: Well, he was doing 60 in a 50 mile –an–hour zone.
   B: Oh.

3.
   A: I really like that car. I bet it's expensive, though.
   B: It's $20,000.
   A: Yeah. That's what I thought. I think I'll probably have to keep looking.

4.
   A: Did you see what happened?
   B: Yeah. The blue car hit the black car from behind.
   A: It was the blue car's fault?
   B: Sure was.

5.
   A: Mom, Bobby's on the phone.
   B: Bobby? What does he want?
   A: His car broke down. You have to get him.

6.
   A: Why is there so much traffic today?
   B: I don't know, but we're going to be late.
   A: Oh, I see what the trouble is.
   B: There's an accident up ahead?
   A: Yeah. Over there. In the left lane.

Exercise 2. Listen. Number the pictures.

Write the number of the conversation that matches each picture.

Conversation 1.

A: What a wreck!
B: You can say that again. The whole front is smashed in.
A: And the sides are all dented. Did you see what happened?
B: Yeah. The driver was pulling out of the parking lot and she didn't see the other car coming from the left.
A: How fast was the other car going?

Conversation 2.

A: It's beautiful. What options does it come with?
B: The usual; air-conditioning, power windows and door locks, AM/FM radio and cassette... Would you like to take it for a test drive?
A: Sure. But we haven't talked price yet. How much is it?

Conversation 3.

A: It looks a little beat up. Was it in an accident?
B: Just a little fender bender. Nothing major.
A: I see. (said skeptically) How many owners has it had?
B: Just one. We're the original owners.
A: And what did you say the mileage on it was?

Conversation 4.

A: Well, considering what happened, things don't look that bad. Besides the broken headlight, there are only a few dents and scratches.
B: What about the engine?
A: I've checked it out and it's fine.
B: Well, go ahead and replace the headlights, but forget about the dents and scratches for now.
A: OK.
B: When do you think it'll be ready?

Exercise 2. Listen again. What do you think the next speaker will say?

Listen to the conversations again. Predict what the next speaker will say.

Exercise 3. You want to travel from Bridgeton to San Diego tomorrow afternoon. Call Caltrack Railways. Use the keypad. Instead of pushing a button, check it. Fill in the information in the boxes.

Welcome to Caltrack Railways automated schedule and fare system. Please have a pencil and paper ready. To begin accessing train schedule information, press 1.

If you are departing from San Francisco, press 1; from Bridgeton, press 2; from Los Angeles, press 3; from San Diego, press 4.

If you are travelling to San Francisco, press 1; to Los Angeles, press 2; to San Diego, press 3.

You are travelling from Bridgeton to San Diego. For train departures today, press 1. For train departures tomorrow, press 2. For train departures on other days, press 3.

For morning departures, press 1. For afternoon departures, press 2. For evening departures, press 3.

The total number of trains for this time period is—three.There's a train leaving at—1:58 p.m.—which will arrive at—8:31 p.m. The train after that leaves at—3:11 p.m.—and arrives at—11:15 p.m. The train after that leaves at—5:11 p.m.—and arrives at—11:56 p.m.

For additional departures, press 1. For fare information, press 2.

The one way unreserved fare for this trip is $65.00.

The round trip excursion fare is $95.00.

To hear train information again, press 1. For additional departures press 2. To end this call, press 3.

Thank you and have a good trip.

UNIT 3   Page 32   Listening Plus.
Exercise 1. Listen to the contrast.

I'll be at the mall at *2:00*.
I'll be at the *mall* at 2:00.

Exercise 1. Point.

Point to *Time* or *Place*.
We're going to the *zoo* at 11:00.
We're going to the *zoo* at 11:00.
We're going to the zoo at *11:00*.
She'll be at the *skating rink* at 1:00.
She'll be at the skating rink at *1:00*.
She'll be at the *skating rink* at 1:00.
They have to be at the stadium at *5:00*.
They have to be at the stadium at *5:00*.
They have to be at the *stadium* at 5:00.
We'll meet you at the *video store* at 6:00.
We'll meet you at the *video store* at 6:00.
We'll meet you at the video store at *6:00*.
We're going to the theater on *Tuesday*.
We're going to the *theater* on Tuesday.
We're going to the *theater* on Tuesday.
I'll pick you up at the pool at *6:00*.
I'll pick you up at the *pool* at 6:00.
I'll pick you up at the *pool* at 6:00.

Exercise 1. Underline the time or place in each sentence.

Look at each sentence in your book. When you hear it in the conversation, underline the time or the place.

1.
A: What time does the movie start?
B: At 9:45.
A: Then we should probably meet at 9:30.
B: That's too late. I'll meet you at the theater at *9:00*. OK?

2.
A: Guess what. I saw Ann at the opera on Friday night.
B: That's not possible.
A: Why not?
B: Ann was at the *movies* Friday night.

3.
A: Any special plans for the weekend?
B: Yeah. my brother's visiting me from out of town and we're going to the beach on Sunday.
A: You're going to the *beach* on Sunday?
B: Uh-huh. It's supposed to be in the 90's.

4.
A: How are you doing, Fred?
B: Fine, Joan. Are we still on for tonight?
A: You bet! We wouldn't miss the fireworks for anything.
B: O.K., then we'll see you at the park at 8:15.
A: Oh, gee. I'm sorry. We may have to wait for our babysitter. We'll see you at the park at *8:30*.

5.
A: Are you ready to go?
B: No! I have to get dressed.
A: Hurry up. We're going to be late.

B: Why? Aren't Meg and Dan coming here at 8:00?
A: No. We're meeting at *Meg's* at 8:00.
B: Oh!

6.
A: Did you hear? I got tickets to the Giants game.
B: Really? That's exciting. When's the game?
A: This Sunday. We're leaving at 11:00.
B: You're leaving for the game at *11:00?*
A: Yes. There's going to be a lot of traffic.

Exercise 2. Listen. Number the pictures.

Write the number of the conversation that matches each picture.

Conversation 1.
A: This is supposed to be really scary.
B: I know. I just hope we get in. Look at all these people!
A: It's too bad we got here so late.
B: *We* didn't get here so late. *You* got here late.
A: Didn't you say, "Meet me at the theater at 7:15"?
B: No. I said, "Meet me at the theater at *7:00.*"

Conversation 2.
A: What kind of movies do you like?
B: Oh, mysteries, comedies...
A: Well, the comedies are right over here. Hey, look at this! It's Sid Baron's latest movie!
B: Did you see it?
A: Yeah. I saw it when it first came out.
B: What did you think of it?

Conversation 3.
A: Can I have some popcorn?
B: Sure. Look at all these people!
A: Yeah. The reviews say it's really a funny movie.
B: Great. I'm in the mood for a good laugh. When's it supposed to begin?

Conversation 4.
A: This is really boring.
B: Oh, I don't know. It's not that bad. Anyway, it'll be over in 15 minutes.
A: Good. Then we can watch something else.
B: OK. What's on?

Exercise 2. Listen again. What do you think the next speaker will say?

Listen to the conversations again. Predict what the next speaker will say.

Exercise 3. Call the *CinemaPhone.* You want information about *Terminator 5* and *Batman 6.* Use the keypad. Instead of pushing a button, check it. Fill in the information in the chart.

Hello and welcome to *CinemaPhone.* If you know the name of the movie you'd like to see, press 1. To select from a list of current movies, press 2. To find out what's playing at a particular theater, press 3. Enter now.

Using your touchtone key pad, please enter the first three letters of the movie title now.

If your selection is *Terminator 5*, press 1. *Test of Courage,* press 2. Or *Very Funny!*, press 3. Enter now.

You have selected *Terminator 5*, rated R.

To find the theaters nearest you showing your movie selection, press 1.

Please enter your five digit ZIP code now.

Your selection, *Terminator 5,* is playing at the

Cinema Six located at Main Street and First Avenue. Today's remaining show times are 12:15, 3:15, 6:15 and 9:15.

To choose another movie, press 1. To end this phone call press 2. Enter now.

If you know the name of the movie you'd like to see, press 1. To select from a list of current movies, press 2. To find out what's playing at a particular theater, press 3. Enter now.

Using your touchtone key pad, please enter the first three letters of the movie title now.

If your selection is *Acting Up*, press 1. *Batman 6*, press 2. Or *Cave of Fear*, press 3. Enter now.

You have selected *Batman 6*, rated PG-13.

To find the theaters nearest you showing your movie selection, press 1.

Please enter your five digit ZIP code now.

Your selection, *Batman 6*, is playing at the Cinema 4 located at Park Street and Avenue A. Today's remaining show times are 1:40, 3:45, 6:00 and 8:10.

To choose another movie, press 1. To end this phone call press 2. Enter now.

Thank you for calling *CinemaPhone*. We hope you enjoy the show!

UNIT 4   Page 44   Listening Plus.

Exercise 1. Listen to the contrast.

She had *German measles* last year.
She had German measles *last year*.

Exercise 1. Point.

Point to *Thing* or *Time*.

She had the *flu* last month.
She had the *flu* last month.
She had the flu *last month*.
She took the pills at *4:00*.
She took the *pills* at 4:00.
She took the *pills* at 4:00.
He got the vaccination in *1991*.
He got the *vaccination* in 1991.
He got the vaccination in *1991*.
I took two *capsules* at dinnertime.
I took two *capsules* at dinnertime.
I took two capsules at *dinnertime*.
He had his appendix removed *last month*.
He had his *appendix* removed last month.
He had his *appendix* removed last month.
She swallowed a *marble* yesterday.
She swallowed a marble *yesterday*.
She swallowed a marble *yesterday*.

Exercise 1. Underline the thing or time in each sentence.

Look at each sentence in your book. When you hear the sentence in the conversation, underline the thing or time.

1.
   A: How's Sally feeling?
   B: Lousy. She didn't sleep at all.
   A: Oh, that's too bad. Did her headache keep her up?
   B: What headache? She had an *earache* last night.

2.
   A: Has Tina ever had the mumps?
   B: No, but she had chicken pox.
   A: What about German measles?
   B: Oh, yes. She had German measles.
   A: When was that? When she was a child?
   B: No. She had German measles *last month*!

3.
   A: What did the doctor say?
   B: The doctor? What do you mean?
   A: Didn't you go to the doctor today?
   B: No. I have an appointment *tomorrow*.
   A: Well, call me when you get home.

4.
   A: How's Johnny?
   B: Not too well. He has another bad cold.
   A: That's too bad. Didn't he just have a cold last week?
   B: He had a cold *last month*.
   A: Oh. It didn't seem that long ago.

5.
   A: Did you remember to take your pills at 9:00?
   B: I took my pills at *10:00*. I'm supposed to take them every four hours, and I took two at 6:00 with dinner.
   A: Oh.

6.
   A: Didn't you have your tonsils removed last year?
   B: I had my *appendix* removed last year. I still have my tonsils.
   A: Maybe that's why you get so many sore throats.
   B: Could be.

Exercise 2. Listen. Number the pictures.

Write the number of the conversation that matches each picture.

Conversation 1.

A: So, Michael. Tell me how you feel.
B: Awful. I have a cough, and my throat hurts.
A: I see. And how long have you had this rash?
B: Just since yesterday. What do you think it is, doctor?

Conversation 2.

A: I'd like to fill this prescription for tetracycline.
B: OK. Have you ever taken tetracycline before?
A: No. But I've had penicillin. Is there any difference?
B: Well, they're both antibiotics, but you're not supposed to take tetracycline with dairy products.
A: I'm sorry?

Conversation 3.

A: Do you want a cup of tea, Tommy?
B: No, thanks, Mom.
A: How are you feeling now?
B: This sore throat is killing me.
A: Oh, I'm sorry, honey.
B: When do I take my pills again?

Conversation 4.

A: There's not too much you can do for German measles. You just have to rest and treat it like a cold.
B: What about the itch?
A: Well, anti-itch cream will help. And here's a prescription for antihistamine.
B: How often do I need to take it?

Exercise 2. Listen again. What do you think the next speaker will say?

Listen to the conversations again. Predict what the next speaker will say.

Exercise 3. Dr. Carson is returning calls. Write down what is wrong with the patient and what the patient should and shouldn't do.

Hello, Mrs. Johnson? This is Doctor Carson. How's Betsy feeling now? (pause) You say her fever's gone down but she still has the rash? Well, you know with chickenpox, it takes some time for the rash to clear up. Just keep giving her children's Tylenol. (pause) That's right. No aspirin. And keep putting the anti-itch cream on the rash. That should help stop the itching. And try to make sure she doesn't scratch. OK? (pause) Good. Call me in three days to let me know how she is. (pause) You're welcome. I hope she feels better. Goodbye. (hang up)

Hello, Mrs. Morgan? This is Doctor Carson returning your call. I understand your husband is running a fever. (pause) 102?. (pause) Uh-huh. (pause) And he's coughing and has a sore throat. I see. Sounds like a bad case of the flu. It's going around now. Well, the best thing is for him to stay in bed and drink lots of liquids. Give him aspirin, too. That should bring down his fever. He can also take some over the counter flu medicine—that'll relieve his cough and other symptoms. (pause) That's right. And if his fever goes up, call me. (pause) OK? (pause) You're welcome. So long. (hang up)

UNIT 5   Page 56   Listening Plus.

Exercise 1. Listen to the contrast.

Can you come on Monday or Tuesday? (choice)
Can you come on Monday or Tuesday? (yes/no)

Exercise 1. Point.

Point to *Choice* or *Yes/No*.

Have you sold TV's or VCR's? (yes/no)
Have you sold TV's or VCR's? (yes/no)
Have you sold TV's or VCR's? (choice)
Can you work the second shift or the third shift? (choice)
Can you work the second shift or the third shift? (yes/no)
Can you work the second shift or the third shift? (choice)
Does he drive a van or a bus? (yes/no)
Does he drive a van or a bus? (choice)
Does he drive a van or a bus? (choice)
Do I fill out an application or send a resume? (choice)
Do I fill out an application or send a resume? (yes/no)
Do I fill out an application or send a resume? (yes/no)
Did Mary or John have an interview? (choice)
Did Mary or John have an interview? (yes/no)
Did Mary or John have an interview? (choice)
Will you call or write? (yes/no)
Will you call or write? (yes/no)
Will you call or write? (choice)

Exercise 1. Write *C* for *Choice* or *Y/N* for *Yes/No.*

Look at each sentence in your book. When you hear the sentence in the conversation, write *C* for *Choice* or *Y/N* for *Yes/No*.

1.
   A: Do you know anything about that new job opening? I have a friend who's looking for work.
   B: New job opening? No. I don't know anything about it. Why don't you ask one of the guys on the fourth floor?
   A: OK. Should I speak to Bob or John? (choice)

2.
   A: I have a job interview tomorrow.
   B: Really? What's the job ?

A: Administrative assistant.

B: Oh. What does an administrative assistant do?

A: You know, answers phones, makes copies, handles correspondence....

B: Oh, like a secretary. Do you type or use a computer? (choice)

3.

A: Hello. I'm calling about the clerical position. Are you interviewing?

B: Not yet. We'll be interviewing next Wednesday. Have you had any experience?

A: Yes. I've been a clerk at Jones and Moore for two years.

B: I see. Would you like an appointment for an interview?

A: Yes, I would. Early morning is best for me.

B: Can you come at 9:00 or 10:00? (yes/no)

4.

A: Did you tell Ken about the order?

B: No. I didn't see him, and he's gone for the day.

A: Well, you'd better leave him a message.

B: OK. Do you have any paper?

A: Here's some. Do you need a pen or a pencil? (yes/no)

5.

A: Hello. I'm calling about your ad in today's paper.

B: Which ad is that?

A: The ad for a computer programmer. Is the job still available?

B: Yes, it is. Do you have a degree or experience? (yes/no)

6.

A: Hi, Phyllis? This is Tony.

B: Oh, hi, Tony. What's up?

A: Well, I just heard about a job opening at my company. They're looking for a new bilingual secretary. I thought you might be interested.

B: Great. Should I call or send a resume? (choice)

Exercise 2. Listen. Number the pictures.

Write the number of the conversation that matches each picture.

Conversation 1.

A: I see from your application that you have a certificate as a nurse's aide.

B: Yes, I got my certificate in 1989.

A: Uh-huh. And now you're working at a nursing home?

B: That's right. The Wavehill Nursing Home.

A: And how long have you been there?

Conversation 2.

A: Hi, Frank. This is Jane.

B: Oh, hi, Jane. How's the job search going?

A: Not great. I keep looking in the paper, but so far, nothing. Any ideas?

B: Well, have you tried an employment agency?

Conversation 3.

A: Conway and Peterson. Good morning.

B: Hello. I'm calling about your ad for a computer operator. Is the position still available?

A: Yes, it is. Would you be able to come in for an interview this week?

B: Sure. When's a good time?

A: Well, can you come in on Tuesday or Wednesday? (yes/no)

Conversation 4.

A: Hi. I'm interested in a job as a salesperson. Are you hiring now?

B: Yes. Here's an application.

A: Thanks.

B: By the way, have you had any experience?

Exercise 2. Listen again. What do you think the next speaker will say?

Listen to the conversations again. Predict what the next speaker will say.

Exercise 3. You're getting directions over the phone to Person Power, an employment agency. Write the directions. Then trace the route on the map.

OK. You're coming from Bridgeton. Take Route 3 south to County Road. Go west on County Road to Route 7. Take Route 7 north to Bank Street. Let's see. Then go west on Bank. When you cross Route 25, Bank becomes Maple Bridge Road. Stay on Maple Bridge to Franklin Boulevard. Turn right. It's the first building on the right.

UNIT 6   Page 68   Listening Plus.

Exercise 1. Listen to the contrast.

Would you like coffee or tea? (choice)
Would you like coffee or tea? (yes/no)

Exercise 1. Point.

Point to *Choice* or *Yes/No.*

Do you want milk or cream? (choice)
Do you want milk or cream? (yes/no)
Do you want milk or cream? (choice)
Did he order the chicken or fish? (yes/no)
Did he order the chicken or fish? (choice)
Did he order the chicken or fish? (choice)
Are they closed on Sunday or Monday? (yes/no)
Are they closed on Sunday or Monday? (choice)
Are they closed on Sunday or Monday? (choice)
Did they add salt or pepper? (yes/no)
Did they add salt or pepper? (yes/no)
Did they add salt or pepper? (choice)
Would you like ketchup or mustard? (choice)
Would you like ketchup or mustard? (yes/no)
Would you like ketchup or mustard? (yes/no)
Did they eat at Gregg's or Carrie's? (yes/no)
Did they eat at Gregg's or Carrie's? (choice)
Did they eat at Gregg's or Carrie's? (choice)

Exercise 1. Write *C* for *Choice* or *Y/N* for *Yes/No.*

Look at each sentence in your book. When you hear the sentence in the conversation, write *C* for *Choice* or *Y/N* for *Yes/No.*

1.

A: Can I get you anything else?

B: Yes. I think I'll have a piece of apple pie.

A: OK. Apple pie. Anything to drink?

B: A cup of tea, please.

A: Would you like milk or lemon? (choice)

2.

A: I'm really hungry.

B: Me too. Let's go out to eat. I'm too tired to cook.

A: Good idea. Where do you want to go?

B: Oh, I don't know. Do you want Mexican or Thai food? (yes/no)

3.

A: Mmmmm. Taste the soup.

B: It's delicious. You can tell it didn't come from a can.

A: I wish I could make soup like this.

B: Me too. Did Janice or Alan make it? (choice)

4.

A: I can't believe the size of this dessert menu. Have you decided what you're going to get?

B: Yeah. I think I'm in the mood for something with chocolate.

A: Hmmm. Sounds good. Will you get the cake or the sundae? (choice)

5.

A: You know, Mary and Joe are coming for dinner Friday night.

B: That's right. What are you going to make?

A: I don't know. They don't eat red meat. Should I make chicken or fish? (yes/no)

6.

A: Have you heard about the new Chinese restaurant?

B: Yeah. It's supposed to be good. We should go there sometime this week.

A: OK. Do you want to go today or Friday? (yes/no)

Exercise 2. Listen. Number the pictures.

Write the number of the conversation that matches each picture.

Conversation 1.

A: Hello. May I help you?

B: Yes. I'd like broiled chicken, mashed potatoes, and green beans.

A: Would you like white meat or dark meat? (choice) You get two pieces.

B: One thigh and one breast, then.

A: Gravy on the mashed potatoes?

B: Sure.

A: OK. Here you are. Be careful. The plate may be hot. Oh, and would you like a dinner roll or French bread? (choice)

Conversation 2.

A: What's the soup of the day?

B: Cream of mushroom.

A: OK. I'll have a cup of that and a hamburger. Make that well-done, please.

B: A cup of soup and a hamburger, well-done. Anything to drink?

A: I'll have coffee, but afterwards.

B: OK. Anything else right now?

Conversation 3.

A: Good evening. Can I help you?

B: Yes. I'll have one Big Burger without the onions or mustard, a large order of fries and a small Coke.

A: That's one Big Burger, hold the onions and mustard, large fries and a small Coke.

B: And how much is that?

Conversation 4.

A: How was everything, sir?

B: Wonderful. Please give my compliments to the chef.

A: Would you like more wine?

B: Oh, no thanks. But I would like some dessert. What do you recommend?

A: Well, the chocolate soufflé is the house specialty.

B: Mmmm. That sounds good.

A: Very good, sir. And would you like coffee or tea? (yes/no)

Listen to the conversations again. Predict what the next speaker will say.

Exercise 3. Customers are calling Luigi's Pizzeria. Take their orders and figure out their checks. Medium pies are $7.50; large pies, $9.50; each topping is $1.00.

Hello, Luigi's Pizzeria. (pause) OK. Your name and address, please? Linda DeMarco. Capital D-E capital M-A-R-C-O? (pause) OK. And you're at 324 Washington. What are the cross streets? (pause) Between 5th and 6th Streets. Uh-huh. And your phone number? (pause) 598... I'm sorry, could you repeat that? (pause) 598-2438. OK. A large pizza? Sure. And what kind of toppings do you want? (pause) Onions, garlic and spinach. OK. (pause) And you want pepperoni, too? OK. Pepperoni. It should take about half an hour, so it'll be delivered around 7:30. (pause) OK. Bye. (hang up)

(phone ringing)

Luigi's Pizzeria. (pause) Your name and address, please? (pause) Oh. You're going to pick it up? OK. I still need your name and phone number. (pause) Joe Mulvaney. How do you spell that? (pause) M-U-L-V-A-N-E-Y? Right. And your number? (pause) 342-4839. OK. A pizza with olives, mushrooms and peppers? (pause) OK. Medium or large? (pause) Medium. (pause) Yes, we can put extra cheese on it, but that'll be $1.00 extra. (pause) Fine, with extra cheese, then. So that's a medium pizza with olives, mushrooms, peppers and extra cheese. (pause) When will it be ready? It'll take about a half an hour, so you can pick it up at around 8:15. (pause) OK. See you then. Bye. (hang up)

UNIT 7   Page 80   Listening Plus.

Exercise 1. Listen to the contrast.

Utilities aren't included.
Utilities *aren't* included.

Exercise 1. Point.

Point to *Unstressed* or *Stressed*.

You can pay by check.
You can pay by check.
You *can* pay by check.
She *didn't* take the apartment.
She didn't take the apartment.
She *didn't* take the apartment.
There *was* a smoke detector.
There *was* a smoke detector.
There was a smoke detector.
The landlord *will* paint.
The landlord will paint.
The landlord will paint.
He *hasn't* decided yet.
He *hasn't* decided yet.
He hasn't decided yet.
Pets *aren't* allowed.
Pets aren't allowed.
Pets *aren't* allowed.

Exercise 1. Underline the auxiliary or *be* only if it is stressed.

Look at each sentence in your book. When you hear it in the conversation, decide if the auxiliary or *be* is stressed. If it is stressed, underline it.

1.
   A: I hear Jane took that apartment on Fifth Street.

B: Yes. In fact, she's moving in next week.
A: Oh. I'm kind of surprised.
B: How come?
A: I thought she was looking for a furnished apartment.
B: It *is* a furnished apartment.

2.
   A: Are you going to take the apartment?
   B: I've decided against it.
   A: Really? How come?
   B: I'd have to get rid of my dog. They don't allow pets.

3.
   A: I heard that Bill and Ann are moving into that new building.
   B: Really? Those apartments are very expensive.
   A: Yeah. I don't know how they're going to do it. They *don't* make a lot of money.

4.
   A: I have to call the landlord tomorrow.
   B: Which landlord? The old one or the new one?
   A: The old one. I hope he'll give us back our security deposit.
   B: Why wouldn't he? The apartment is in perfect condition.

5.
   A: Thanks for coming over. I really need help with this wiring.
   B: No problem. Gee, it's a little cold in here. Is there a window open?
   A: No. The furnace is broken. The repair guy hasn't shown up yet.

6.
   A: When did Mara sign the lease?
   B: She didn't sign the lease.
   A: You're kidding! How come?
   B: She decided not to move after all. It's just too expensive.

Exercise 2. Listen. Number the pictures.

Write the number of the conversation that matches each picture.

Conversation 1.

A: As you can see, everything's brand new.
B: It certainly looks nice. Mind if I open the cabinets?
A: No, not at all. Go ahead.
B: Hmmm. An electric range... That reminds me... Are utilities included?

Conversation 2.

A: How's the water pressure?
B: It's pretty strong.
A: That's good. In *my* apartment it's so weak I never seem to be able to get the shampoo out of my hair.
B: You won't have that problem here. Well, now that you've seen the whole apartment, what do you think?
A: I like it. When will it be available?

Conversation 3.

A: Gee, it's nice and bright.
B: Yeah, it's great for plants.
A: That's just what I was thinking. I was picturing my sofa over here and my plants over there. By the way, are pets allowed?

Conversation 4.

A: Is it quiet at night? I can't sleep if it's noisy.
B: Well, it faces the back so you really can't hear any street noise.
A: That's good. Now you said the rent's $535. What about the security deposit?

Exercise 2. Listen again. What do you think the next speaker will say?

Listen to the conversations again. Predict what the next speaker will say.

Exercise 3. You're calling the Recycling Center for information. You live downtown. For each category, write an example of something you can recycle and complete the notes.

Welcome to the Community Recycling Program. To clean up our environment, let's all pitch in and recycle. All glass food and beverage containers are recyclable. These include spaghetti sauce jars, baby food jars and juice bottles. Metal caps and rings are OK.

Food and beverage cans are also recyclable. These include soda cans, vegetable cans and pet food cans. Paint cans and cans containing household cleaning products are *not* recyclable.

All plastic beverage containers are recyclable. These include milk, water and juice bottles. Please remove caps and step on the bottles to flatten them.

Remember: Only clean containers can be recycled.

All newspapers can be recycled. Magazines and telephone books are not recyclable at this time.

Put your recyclables in the blue bin provided by the city. Please tie string around newspapers or place them in a brown paper bag on top of or beside your recycling bin.

Place your bin at the curb in front of your house by 6:00 a.m. on your collection day.

Collection days are as follows:

If you live in Bridgeton Heights, collection is on Tuesdays.

If you live in Mountainview, collection is on Thursdays.

If you live Downtown, collection is on Mondays.

If you live in Ferndale, collection is on Wednesdays.

For further information, please call 734-2335.

Remember: Together we can build a better, brighter future. Start recycling today!

UNIT 8   Page 92   Listening Plus.

Exercise 1. Listen to the contrast.

People have been complaining.
People *have* been complaining.

Exercise 1. Point.

Point to *Unstressed* or *Stressed*.
It *hasn't* been working.
It *hasn't* been working.
It hasn't been working.
She *is* the manager.
She *is* the manager.
She's the manager.
Sam was late.
Sam *was* late.
Sam *was* late.
She *can* fire you.
She can fire you.
She *can* fire you.
You *don't* need approval.
You *don't* need approval.
You don't need approval.
The drawer's been jamming.
The drawer *has* been jamming.
The drawer *has* been jamming.

Exercise 1. Underline the auxiliary or *be* only if it is stressed.

Look at each sentence in your book. When you hear it in the conversation, decide if the auxiliary or *be* is stressed. If it is stressed, underline it.

1.
- A: Have you decided when you're going to take your vacation?
- B: Yes. I'm going to take off the first week in March.
- A: Have you put in a request yet?
- B: Well, I mentioned it to Sandy.
- A: That's not enough. You should put it in writing.

2.
- A: Eric. It's 9:15. You're late again.
- B: I know. I just can't seem to get up in the morning. Is Mr. Johnson in yet?
- A: Yes. And he's been asking for you.
- B: Well, I'm only 15 minutes late.
- A: Yeah. But watch it. You can get fired for that.

3.
- A: What's the matter, Paula?
- B: Oh, I'm just frustrated. I need to speak to Christine, and she hasn't called me back.
- A: Maybe you should call her again.
- B: I *can't* call her. She's out seeing clients today.

4.
- A: Mary forgot to ship the package today.
- B: Oh, really? Did you speak to her about it?
- A: Yes, but I'm afraid she'll never learn.
- B: C'mon. Give her a break. She hasn't been working here long.

5.
- A: Hey, Joan! Come here. The air conditioner is leaking.
- B: What! You're kidding! Let me see.
- A: I thought the guy was coming to fix it.
- B: He *was* coming. But then I called him back and told him to forget it. I thought it was OK.

6.
- A: I don't understand this.
- B: What's the problem?
- A: Well, I just went up to the Personnel Office to sign up for the health insurance plan, and they said I wasn't eligible.
- B: You *aren't* eligible. You haven't worked here for three months.
- A: Three months? Oh, I thought you only had to be here two months.

Exercise 2. Listen. Number the pictures.

Write the number of the conversation that matches each picture.

Conversation 1.

A: Do you need some help?
B: Yeah, thanks. Could you get the door?
A: Sure. That looks heavy.
B: Yup. It is.
A: It's a good thing your hands are protected. Looks like you could get splinters carrying that.
B: Uh huh.
A: By the way, where are you going to put it?

Conversation 2.

A: Do you have any questions?

B: No. I think I've got it. I push this button down when I'm ready to start.
A: Right. And don't forget to wear these. You need them to protect your eyes.
B: Thanks. Can I put them over my glasses?

Conversation 3.

A: What happened?
B: Oh. The tool box just fell off the bench.
A: Did you get hurt?
B: No, but it's a good thing I was wearing these.
A: Yeah, someone broke their toe last week.
B: I heard. I have to get a new pair, though. These are getting old. Where did you get yours?

Conversation 4.

A: Remember. You have to wear these whenever you're in the work area.
B: Gee, it's going to be hot wearing those.
A: Yeah, but it's better to be hot than to risk injury. These could save your lives if something falls from up there and lands on your head.
B: I suppose so.
A: OK, guys, let's go. Say, John, where are your work gloves?

Exercise 2. Listen again. What do you think the next speaker will say?

Listen to the conversations again. Predict what the next speaker will say.

Exercise 3. You're an administrative assistant at Prince Fabrics, Inc. Your boss is out of the office today. He has dictated a memo on your office answering machine. Write the memo.

Hi. This is Ken. I forgot to give you this memo to do before I left the office. It's about the Thanksgiving holiday. It goes to all employees. Are you ready? Here goes:

(dictated at a slower, more deliberate speed)

"The office will close at 3:00 tomorrow, November 25. I hope you and your family have a Happy Thanksgiving. See you on Monday."

(back to normal conversational speed)

Got it? Please make sure you get it out right away. Thanks a lot. Have a good holiday. (hang up)

UNIT 9   Page 104   Listening Plus.

Exercise 1. Listen to the contrast.

They have good prices, don't they? (rising)
They have good prices, don't they? (falling)

Exercise 1. Point.

Point to *Question* or *Comment*.

It's on sale, isn't it? (falling)
It's on sale, isn't it? (rising)
It's on sale, isn't it? (falling)
They don't give refunds, do they? (rising)
They don't give refunds, do they? (falling)
They don't give refunds, do they? (falling)
They're guaranteed, aren't they? (falling)
They're guaranteed, aren't they? (rising)
They're guaranteed, aren't they? (rising)
Sands opens at 9:00, doesn't it? (rising)
Sands opens at 9:00, doesn't it? (falling)
Sands opens at 9:00, doesn't it? (rising)
They don't carry small sizes, do they? (falling)
They don't carry small sizes, do they? (rising)
They don't carry small sizes, do they? (rising)
That's the wrong size, isn't it? (falling)
That's the wrong size, isn't it? (falling)
That's the wrong size, isn't it? (rising)

Exercise 1. Write *Q* for *Question* and *C* for *Comment*.

Look at each sentence in your book. When you hear it in the conversation, decide if the sentence is a question or a comment. Write *Q* for *Question* or *C* for *Comment*.

1.
- A: Look at these blouses. They're on sale.
- B: How much are they?
- A: $15.98, and they're 100% silk.
- B: That's a good price, isn't it? (falling) Maybe you should buy a few.

2.
- A: We need a new vacuum cleaner. Our old one keeps breaking down. Wanna come to Plymouth's with me?
- B: OK. What time do you wanna go?
- A: Oh, around seven. They're open late, aren't they? (rising)
- B: Uh-huh. I think they're open 'til 9:00. That'll give us plenty of time to eat dinner first.

3.
- A: That'll be $28.95
- B: Here's $30.
- A: OK. And here's your change.
- B: By the way, I'm getting this as a gift. You give refunds, don't you? (rising)
- A: Yes. As long as you save the receipt.

4.
- A: That's a nice sweater. How much is it?
- B: Eighty dollars.
- A: It's expensive, isn't it? (falling) Maybe we should wait and see if it goes on sale.

5.
- A: What did you do on the weekend, Pam?
- B: I went shopping at the new mall. Have you been there yet?
- A: No. It's on Route 4, isn't it? (rising)
- B: Yeah. Right before the Branch Avenue exit.

6.
- A: Did I tell you about what happened to me last week?
- B: No. What?
- A: Well, I was shopping in Sands and someone picked my pocket.
- B: That's terrible! That happened to Al, too, didn't it? (rising)
- A: Yeah. He, was lucky, though. They caught the guy.

Exercise 2. Listen. Number the pictures.

Write the number of the conversation that matches each picture.

Conversation 1.

A: That'll be $19.95.
B: OK. One second, please.
A: Certainly... Um, I'll need some form of ID for that.
B: Is a driver's license OK?
A: Yes. That'll be fine.
B: And who should I make it out to?

Conversation 2.

A: That's $14.50. Here's your change. That's 15... ...and 5 makes 20. And here's your receipt.
B: OK. And if I want to exchange it, how many days do I have?

Conversation 3.

A: Just sign here, please.
B: I'm sorry. Where?
A: Right here. Next to the X.

B: Oh, I see. Thanks. And where can I get a gift box for this?

Conversation 4.

A: This was a gift and it didn't fit.

B: I see. Do you have the receipt?

A: No. I'm sorry, I don't. But the tags are still on.

B: That's fine. Would you like to exchange it for another size or would you prefer a store credit?

A: Oh. Can't I get cash?

Exercise 2. Listen again. What do you think the next speaker will say?

Listen to the conversations again. Predict what the next speaker will say.

Exercise 3. Call Sands department store for information about your Sands charge account. Use the keypad. Instead of pushing a button, check it. Your account number is 14-311-23-616.

Thank you for calling Sands Department Store. Located at the Lincoln Mall, Sands is open Monday through Saturday from 10 a.m. to 9:30 p.m., and Sunday from 11 a.m to 6:00 p.m.

If you are calling from a rotary phone, please hold and the next available operator will be happy to assist you.

If you are calling from a touchtone phone, for faster service, please press 1 now.

If you know the extension of the person or the department you are trying to reach, please enter the four digit number now. If you would like information regarding your Sands account or to report a lost or stolen credit card, please press 2 now.

Thank you. Just a moment.

Thank you for calling Sands Credit Services. You have reached the Status Line. If you would like account information, and if you have your account number, please press 1. If you want information on where to mail your payment, please press 2. If you have questions regarding merchandise or store service, please press 3. To report a lost or stolen credit card, please press 4.

Please enter your account number followed by the pound sign, now.

Thank you. Please hold while I get your account information.

Your available credit is: 1,211 dollars.

The balance on your account as of yesterday was: 289 dollars and 36 cents.

The last payment we received was on: May 28.

For information on another account, please press 1, now.

To end this call please press 9 now.

Thank you for calling Sands Credit Services. We appreciate the opportunity to serve you.

UNIT 10   Page 116   Listening Plus.

Exercise 1. Listen to the contrast.

It isn't open, is it? (rising)
It isn't open, is it? (falling)

Exercise 1. Point.

Point to *Question* or *Comment*.

The Post Office won't be open today, will it? (falling)
The Post Office won't be open today, will it? (rising)
The Post Office won't be open today, will it? (rising)

The class is free, isn't it? (rising)
The class is free, isn't it? (falling)
The class is free, isn't it? (falling)
They haven't gotten their licenses yet, have they? (falling)
They haven't gotten their licenses yet, have they? (rising)
They haven't gotten their licenses yet, have they? (rising)
You need a library card, don't you? (falling)
You need a library card, don't you? (falling)
You need a library card, don't you? (rising)
There's a late fee, isn't there? (falling)
There's a late fee, isn't there? (rising)
There's a late fee, isn't there? (rising)
You can borrow video tapes, can't you? (falling)
You can borrow video tapes, can't you? (falling)
You can borrow video tapes, can't you? (rising)

Exercise 1. Write Q for *Question* or C for *Comment*.

Look at each sentence in your book. When you hear it in the conversation, decide if the sentence is a question or a comment. Write *Q* for *Question* or *C* for *Comment*.

1.
A: Your post office is much better than mine.
B: Really? How come?
A: Well, it doesn't seem crowded, and the clerks are really helpful.
B: Yeah. They're fast, too, aren't they? (falling)

2.
A: Are you going to the concert in the park?
B: When is it?
A: Thursday night. The Red Hots are playing.
B: Sounds good. It's free, isn't it? (falling)
A: Uh-huh. And it usually gets pretty crowded. So it's a good idea to get there early.

3.
A: I'm going to the mall to have my blood pressure taken.
B: The mall?
A: Yes. The Red Cross is doing free blood pressure screening all day.
B: Oh! Maybe I'll go too. What about an appointment? You don't need one, do you? (rising)
A: No. It's first come, first served.

4.
A: Look at that building! It's on fire!
B: Quick! There's a phone. Let's call the fire department.
A: What's the number?
B: It's 911. It's 911 everywhere, isn't it? (rising)

5.
A: How's your report going, Ed?
B: It's OK, but I don't have all the information I need. I really need to use an encyclopedia.
A: Why don't you go to the library. You can use one there, can't you? (rising)
B: Yeah. But it's not open now.

6.
A: Oh, are you borrowing that video?
B: Uh-huh. It's supposed to be really good. I just read the book.
A: So did I. It was great, wasn't it? (falling)
B: Yeah. I'm curious to see how they did the movie.

Exercise 2. Listen. Number the pictures.

Write the number of the conversation that matches each picture.

Conversation 1.

A: I'd like to check this out.
B: Oh. I'm sorry. You're not allowed to take that out of the library.
A: Oh, no! I have to work on this report over the weekend.
B: Well, if you like, you can make photocopies of the pages you need.
A: Oh. OK. Thanks. Can you tell me where the photocopier is?

Conversation 2.

A: OK. That'll be one dollar.
B: A dollar? How come? I thought it was free.
A: Most videos are. But this is a new release. They're a dollar.
B: Oh. And when is it due?

Conversation 3.

A: I'm sorry, ma'am, but these are overdue.
B: They are?
A: Yes. They were due on the 21st and today's the 24th.
B: Oh, I'm sorry. I didn't realize that. How much do I owe you?

Conversation 4

A: I can return this here, can't I? (rising)
B: No. I'm sorry. You have to take it back to the Downtown Branch.
A: Really? I thought I could return it to any branch.
B: No. That's only true for books. Everything else has to go back to the branch you borrowed it from.
A: I see. What time does the Downtown Branch close today?

Exercise 2. Listen again. What do you think the next speaker will say?

Listen to the conversations again. Predict what the next speaker will say.

Exercise 3. Call the Bridgeton Public Library. Get information and take notes.

This is the Downtown Branch of the Bridgeton Public Library, located at 22 Jefferson Street. Our hours are Monday through Thursday 10:00 a.m. to 8:55 p.m. Friday and Saturday 10:00 a.m. to 5:55 p.m., and Sundays from noon to 5:55 p.m.. We are closed on holidays. For information regarding overdue books or fines, please call 489-2021. For reference questions, please call information services at 489-2043 or 489-2050. For the Children's Library, please call 489-2035.

(slight pause)

This is the Downtown Branch of the Bridgeton Public Library, located at 22 Jefferson Street. Our hours are Monday through Thursday 10:00 a.m. to 8:55 p.m. Friday and Saturday 10:00 a.m. to 5:55 p.m., and Sundays from noon to 5:55 p.m.. We are closed on holidays. For information regarding overdue books or fines, please call 489-2021. For reference questions, please call information services at 489-2043 or 489-2050. For the Children's Library, please call 489-2035.

(slight pause)

This is the Downtown Branch of the Bridgeton Public Library, located at 22 Jefferson Street. Our hours are Monday through Thursday 10:00 a.m. to 8:55 p.m. Friday and Saturday 10:00 a.m. to 5:55 p.m., and Sundays from noon to 5:55 p.m. We are closed on holidays. For information regarding overdue books or

(disconnect sound)

Basic Conversations
for Progress Checks: *What are the people saying?*
(These are suggested answers. Students' answers will vary.)

Unit 1

2. A: Hello, my name is *(female name)*.
   B: I'm Doug Powell.
   A: I'm sorry. What was your name?
   B: Doug Powell.
   A: Doug, I'd like you to meet *(female name)*. *(Female name)*, I'd like you to meet Doug Powell.
   B: Nice to meet you.
   C: Nice to meet you, too.

3. A: Where are you from?
   B: I'm from Mexico.
   A: What did you do there?
   B: I was a teacher.
   A: When did you come to the United States?
   B: Six years ago.

Unit 2

1. A: What happened?
   B: The gray car was going east on Fourth Avenue when the white car went through a traffic light and crashed into it.
   A: How fast was the gray car going?
   B: Thirty-five miles an hour.

Unit 3

2. A: What kind of movies do you like?
   B: I like comedies and love stories. What about you?
   A: I like comedies and action movies.
   B: Gee, it's getting late. I'll see you tomorrow.
   A: OK. See you.

3. A: What do you want to do next Saturday night?
   B: How about going bowling?
   A: What time are you free?
   B: Around 7:00 p.m.
   A: OK. So we'll go bowling at the Olympia at 7:00 p.m. on Saturday.
   B: Great.

Unit 4

2. A: Take this with food.
   B: Excuse me?
   A: You're supposed to eat something when you take this medicine.

3. A: What's the problem?
   B: My son has a rash.
   A: Has he ever had chicken pox?
   B: No, he hasn't.

Unit 5

2. A: Hello. I'm calling about the job as a secretary. Is it still available?
   B: Yes, it is.
   A: Is it full time?
   B: No, it isn't. *(Students should continue the conversation.)*

3. A: Hello, this is *(name)*. I applied for the job as a secretary. I was wondering . . . Have you reviewed my application?
   B: Yes, we have. Would you be available for an interview Monday or Tuesday?

Unit 6

2. A: How did you find class tonight?
   B: It was tough.
   A: Yeah, I know what you mean.
   B: By the way, do you have any plans for next Friday night? I'm having a party.

Unit 7

1. A: I'm looking for a two-bedroom apartment.
   B: We have a nice two-bedroom in Bridgeton Heights.
   A: What's it like?
   B: It's on the first floor, and it has a large modern kitchen.
   A: How much is the rent?
   B: It's $560 a month.

Unit 8

1. A: What's the problem?
   B: This drawer has been jamming all morning.

3. A: I'm giving you two week's notice. I've accepted another job.
   B: I'm sorry to hear that. When is your last day?

There are no suggested conversations for Units 9 and 10.

Useful Irregular Verbs

Base Form	Past Form	Perfect Form
become	became	become
begin	began	begun
bend	bent	bent
bet	bet	bet
bid	bid	bid
bite	bit	bitten
bleed	bled	bled
blow	blew	blown
break	broke	broken
bring	brought	brought
build	built	built
buy	bought	bought
catch	caught	caught
choose	chose	chosen
come	came	come
cost	cost	cost
cut	cut	cut
do	did	done
draw	drew	drawn
drink	drank	drunk
drive	drove	driven
eat	ate	eaten
fall	fell	fallen
feed	fed	fed
feel	felt	felt
fight	fought	fought
find	found	found
fly	flew	flown
forget	forgot	forgotten
freeze	froze	frozen
get	got	gotten
give	gave	given
go	went	gone
grow	grew	grown
hang	hung	hung
hear	heard	heard
hide	hid	hidden
hit	hit	hit
hold	held	held
hurt	hurt	hurt
keep	kept	kept
know	knew	known
lay	laid	laid
lead	led	led
leave	left	left
lend	lent	lent
let	let	let
lie	lay	lain

Base Form	Past Form	Perfect Form
light	lit	lit
lose	lost	lost
make	made	made
mean	meant	meant
meet	met	met
pay	paid	paid
put	put	put
quit	quit	quit
read	read	read
ride	rode	ridden
ring	rang	rung
rise	rose	risen
run	ran	run
say	said	said
see	saw	seen
sell	sold	sold
send	sent	sent
shake	shook	shaken
shine	shone	shone
shoot	shot	shot
shrink	shrank	shrunk
shut	shut	shut
sing	sang	sung
sit	sat	sat
sleep	slept	slept
speak	spoke	spoken
spend	spent	spent
stand	stood	stood
steal	stole	stolen
stick	stuck	stuck
stink	stank	stunk
strike	struck	struck
swear	swore	sworn
sweep	swept	swept
swell	swelled	swollen
swim	swam	swum
take	took	taken
teach	taught	taught
tear	tore	torn
tell	told	told
think	thought	thought
throw	threw	thrown
understand	understood	understood
wake	woke	woken
wear	wore	worn
win	won	won
write	wrote	written